Guardians of the Next Generation

Other Books by Nicholas D. Young

Achieving Results: Maximizing Student Success in the Schoolhouse

Betwixt and Between: Understanding and Meeting the Social and Emotional Development Needs of Students during the Middle School Transition Years

Beyond the Bedtime Story: Promoting Reading Development during the Middle School Years

Captivating Classrooms: Student Engagement at the Heart of School Improvement

Educational Entrepreneurship: Promoting Public-Private Partnerships for the 21st Century

Embracing and Educating the Autistic Child: Valuing Those Who Color Outside the Lines (in-press)

From Cradle to Classroom: A Guide to Special Education for Young Children

From Floundering to Fluent: Reaching and Teaching Struggling Readers

Making the Grade: Promoting Positive Outcomes for Students with Learning Disabilities

Paving the Pathway for Educational Success: Effective Classroom Strategies for Students with Learning Disabilities

Soul of the Schoolhouse: Cultivating Student Engagement (in-press)

Transforming Special Education Practices: A Primer for School Administrators and Policy Makers

Wrestling with Writing: Instructional Strategies for Struggling Students

Guardians of the Next Generation

Igniting the Passion for High-Quality Teaching

Nicholas D. Young, Kristen Bonanno-Sotiropoulos, and Jennifer A. Smolinski

ROWMAN & LITTLEFIELD
Lanham • Boulder • New York • London

Published by Rowman & Littlefield
An imprint of The Rowman & Littlefield Publishing Group, Inc.
4501 Forbes Boulevard, Suite 200, Lanham, Maryland 20706
www.rowman.com

Unit A, Whitacre Mews, 26-34 Stannary Street, London SE11 4AB

Copyright © 2018 by Nicholas D. Young, Kristen Bonanno-Sotiropoulos, and Jennifer A. Smolinski

All rights reserved. No part of this book may be reproduced in any form or by any electronic or mechanical means, including information storage and retrieval systems, without written permission from the publisher, except by a reviewer who may quote passages in a review.

British Library Cataloguing in Publication Information Available

Library of Congress Cataloging-in-Publication Data Is Available

ISBN 978-1-4758-4329-3 (cloth: alk. paper)
ISBN 978-1-4758-4330-9 (pbk: alk. paper)
ISBN 978-1-4758-4331-6 (electronic)

∞ ™ The paper used in this publication meets the minimum requirements of American National Standard for Information Sciences Permanence of Paper for Printed Library Materials, ANSI/NISO Z39.48-1992.

Printed in the United States of America

I wish to dedicate my contributions to this book to the teachers I have worked closely with in the Springfield Public Schools, the Monson Public Schools, the Gateway Public Schools, the Hadley Public Schools, and the South Hadley Public Schools. They have demonstrated extraordinary commitment to their students and have truly modeled what it means to be guardians of the next generation. I consider myself privileged to have spent my career alongside theirs.

—**Nicholas D. Young**

I dedicate my portion of this book to my daughters, Emma, Laura, and Audrey. I am proud of many accomplishments in my life, but nothing comes close to being your mom! I love you all!

—**Kristen Bonanno-Sotiropoulos**

I would like to dedicate my portion of this book to all the educators who have inspired me to continue on the path of knowledge and scholarship.

—**Jennifer Smolinski**

Contents

Preface		ix
Acknowledgments		xv
1	Preservice to Practice: Preparing Teachers to Make a Difference	1
2	Collaboration Is Key: Embracing Meaningful Teamwork	11
3	The Home-School Connection: Promoting and Sustaining Successful Partnerships	19
4	Positive Classroom Management: Establishing Beneficial Expectations and Norms	29
5	Effective Instruction: Evidence-Based and High-Quality Practices	37
6	Promoting Student Engagement: Setting the Conditions for Success	47
7	Using Assessment Wisely: Creating, Analyzing, and Moving Forward from Data	55
8	Teaching the Whole Child: The Importance of Social-Emotional Learning	65
9	Potent Administrative Practices: Empowering Teachers to Foster Student Achievement	75
10	Integrating Technology, Teaching, and Learning: Changing with the Times	87
11	Making Professional Development Meaningful: Promising Approaches and Practices	95
12	Keeping Teachers on the Straight and Narrow: Understanding the Fundamentals of School Law	107

References 119
About the Authors 131

Preface

Ask teachers why they have pursued a career in education and they are likely to mention a strong desire to make a difference in the lives of children or suggest that teaching was a calling not just a job. Research shows that in addition to these reasons, teachers also indicated that they joined the academic ranks to share a deep interest in a particular subject area, to work with students of different backgrounds and abilities, or to engage students in creative ways (Lambert, 2018; Westervelt, 2016). For these reasons, and many more, *Guardians of the Next Generation: Igniting the Passion for High-Quality Teaching Practices,* addresses the very heart of what helps teachers to make learning meaningful to children.

Written for preservice and veteran educators, special education and general education teachers, school administrators and college professors, as well as school guidance counselors and parents, this book examines topics such as collaboration, home-school partnerships, instruction, and social-emotional learning. In addition to high-quality teaching strategies and evidence-based practices, the authors take a deep look at technology efforts and professional development initiatives, as well as administrative practices and teacher leadership roles. These are not easy tasks and, as such, all those involved in the education of young people need to ensure they are ready to take on the challenge.

Our motivation for writing this book comes from a number of concerns:

- Our awareness that the field of education has become more difficult due to rigorous state standards, a diversified student population, and a lack of highly qualified teachers in demanding content areas such as special education, bilingual education, math, and science (Westervelt, 2016);

- Our concern that 8% of teachers leave the field annually and 40–50% of new teachers will leave the profession within five years, mostly due to burnout (Crowell, 2017; Westervelt, 2016);
- Our understanding that creating successful home-school partnerships is a necessary step in helping our nation's students find success in the classroom;
- Our knowledge that teacher buy-in is greatest when there is an investment in consistent, meaningful professional development and teachers feel supported and are given autonomy; and,
- Our commitment to identifying and sharing both high-quality teaching strategies and evidence-based teaching practices that lead to greater student engagement and academic achievement for all students.

Teachers share knowledge and tools with students so that they can be successful academically, socially, and emotionally, in school and beyond (Meador, 2017f). Often, teachers must accomplish these goals in harmony with meeting state and district standards and policies, with limited resources, in over-crowded classrooms, and with extremely diverse student populations (Lambert, 2018; Westervelt, 2016). The pressure to fulfill an educational agenda that meets those criteria is extreme; however, there are well-researched methods and strategies that support, nurture, and increase teacher effectiveness in many ways (Alber, 2015; Marzano, Frontier, & Livingston, 2011).

Today's teachers are not as diverse a population as one might think. According to the National Center for Educational Statistics (2014), the average teacher is over the age of 40 (44%), female (56%), and has earned at least a master's degree or higher. The average educator teaches in a classroom with a class size of approximately 24 students and has an average salary of $55,000 (U.S. Bureau of Labor Statistics, 2016a, 2016b).

Vilorio (2016) identified reasons for becoming an educator as well as a list meant to discourage a career in teaching. On the list of positives, teachers mentioned such things as watching students succeed, getting to know students, and working with similarly minded people who value education, while the negative aspects included classroom management; long hours; budgetary cuts; too much student testing; and frustration with local, state, and federal oversights (Meador, 2017a).

Lambert (2018) supported the notion of too much testing but also acknowledged additional challenges to the teaching profession that included too many new initiatives without sufficient time to see change, using students as data only, and not acknowledging students for who they really are—children.

It is predicted that the United States will need 1.9 million teachers over the next six years yet, teacher shortages and college program retention issues continue to remain a valid concern (Camera, 2016; Lambert, 2018). Nearly double the number of teachers leave the teaching profession every year, as compared to other countries and, as a result, the hiring of uncredentialed teachers to fill empty positions has become part of the "norm" (Camera, 2016; Westervelt, 2016).

Unfortunately, these positions are in high-needs areas such as special education, bilingual education, math, and science in which well-prepared individuals are needed most (Camera, 2016). Equally important, high-poverty schools and districts experience the highest rates of teacher attrition and shortages; for example, there is a 90% shortage of special education teachers in high-poverty districts compared to 50% in all other districts (Westervelt, 2016). Further statistics revealed that 1 in 5 teachers within high-poverty schools are unprepared to teach the students before them (Westervelt, 2016).

Research suggested that when teachers are supported, especially new teachers, they tend to stay in the profession longer (Meador, 2017f). Support can be provided in many ways, such as mentoring or coaching relationships, collaborative activities, and meaningful professional development opportunities (Lambert, 2018; Meador, 2017f). Camera (2016) suggested that policy makers focus too much on supporting teacher preparation programs and instead should offer more assistance addressing the poor working conditions many teachers face.

In years past, becoming a teacher was somewhat easy; however, with the increase in learning and teaching expectations for both students and teachers, the requirements to become an educator have increased drastically (Weller, 2017). Teacher candidates must obtain at least a bachelor's degree and pass rigorous and extensive state licensing exams, then they must stay current in the latest teaching methodologies and evidence-based practices (Weller, 2017). It is through further schooling and meaningful professional development opportunities that this occurs.

In 2016, there were approximately 200,000 teacher candidates enrolled in teacher preparation programs, and yet upon graduation, 62% of new teachers felt unprepared to enter into a career as a classroom teacher (Aragon, 2016). In addition, there was a 35% decrease in the enrollment in teacher preparation programs across the country (Aragon, 2016; Camera, 2016; Westervelt, 2016).

Further statistics revealed that only 23% of teacher preparation graduates were from the top third of their class and only 14% of teachers in high-poverty districts graduated in the top third of their teacher preparation program (Aragon, 2016). Another alarming statistic revealed by Lambert (2018) suggested that 40% of undergraduate teacher candidates had never even entered the classroom. Finally, Westervelt (2016) revealed that teachers earned 20% less than other similarly educated college graduates.

The goal of any teacher preparation program should be to recruit, select, and prepare teachers to be hired, retained, and able to produce academic results for all students (Aragon, 2016). The strongest teacher preparation programs engage in extensive and rigorous clinical experiences (Lambert, 2018; Aragon, 2016). The Department of Education (as cited in Aragon, 2016) identified several ways in which teacher preparation programs could strengthen the abilities of their teacher candidates, therefore ensuring a stable and growth-minded teaching workforce.

Included in the list were teacher preparation programs that identify and implement heightened entry and exit standards for teacher candidates, redesign programs to include highly clinical-based courses and field-based experiences, include extensive training in research-based instructional practices, and increase partnerships with local school districts (Aragon, 2016). These should be accomplished in conjunction with a passing grade on rigorous state exams that are meant to influence the face of education in a positive way (Lambert, 2018).

Attracting and retaining highly qualified teachers should be the goal of most school districts (Pickens, 2015). Once schools have recruited highly effective teachers, they must work hard to ensure teacher burnout does not occur. According to Pickens (2015), teacher burnout includes emotional exhaustion, feelings of disconnect, difficulty in feeling accomplished, and being incapable of fulfilling teaching responsibilities. When teachers receive ongoing support by administrators, coworkers, and families, it builds mentally healthy teachers, which in turn produces emotionally healthy students (Pickens, 2015).

Research suggested that the biggest way to support and retain teachers is to work to change poor working conditions (Camera, 2016; Pickens, 2015; Westervelt, 2016). Poor working conditions such as budget cuts, lack of resources, large class sizes, isolation, and decreased administrative support contribute to teacher burnout and attrition rates (Westervelt, 2016; Camera, 2016). Teachers are often provided with scripted curriculums that teach to a test; they have less autonomy in their classrooms and feel increased pressure to have all of their students meet state standards despite diverse abilities (Westervelt, 2016). It is important to address the negative influences and change the culture of education in order to improve teacher and student outcomes.

Written by a team of educational professionals, this book provides administrators with the research and knowledge necessary to support teachers who work tirelessly to increase student achievement for all types of learners, while offering study results, strategies, and practices to preservice and professional educators to become highly effective teachers. Through these pages, the reader will gain valuable awareness and insight into extensive research-based practices that support high-quality teaching. It is our hope that this book will be well used as the educator, administrator, or parent finds new helpful information to increase the success of the students around them.

Acknowledgments

It is with deep appreciation that we thank Suzanne Clark for her editorial assistance on this book project. Her contributions made it far better, and we are grateful.

Chapter One

Preservice to Practice

Preparing Teachers to Make a Difference

All children are entitled to a great teacher, and having a teacher who can provide a world-class education is critical for their success, particularly in high-need communities (National Council for Accreditation of Teacher Education, 2014). Research has demonstrated that well-prepared teachers not only produce higher student achievement and generate 5–6 more months of student learning each year but also are more likely to remain in teaching (National Council for Accreditation of Teacher Education, 2014). Studies on unprepared and underprepared teachers versus fully prepared teachers consistently show that the students of teachers who are prepared show stronger learning gains (National Council for Accreditation of Teacher Education, 2014).

To better meet the needs of students today, expectations for teachers continue to rise, while funding for schools is on the decline, and teachers are expected to do more with less (Horvath & Caulfield, 2016). In the meantime, the preschool to 12th grade (P12) student population is increasing, retirement rates are rising, high attrition rates and diminished interests in teaching are occurring, and all are leading to a shortage of licensed teaching professionals (Horvath & Caulfield, 2016). As a result, there has been a gradual and uneven lowering of the minimum requirements for entry into the teaching profession and more teachers are entering the profession unprepared and vastly inexperienced (Horvath & Caulfield, 2016).

TEACHER PREPARATION REGULATIONS

Teacher preparation regulations are designed to ensure that inexperienced teachers are ready to succeed in the classroom and that all students are taught by skilled educators (U.S. Department of Education, 2016a). Recent regulations seek to provide ongoing feedback to help programs strive for continuous improvement and respond to educators across the country who feel unprepared to enter the classroom (U.S. Department of Education, 2016a). In order to meet the myriad needs found in today's classrooms and to compete with educational standards worldwide, it is imperative to provide our future educators with strong and diverse preparation programs that will generate a steady flow of new teachers with the right mix of knowledge and skills (U.S. Department of Education, 2016a).

The rules for teacher preparation programs focus on promoting stronger outcomes for all programs while giving states significant flexibility in how they measure program performance to reflect both local needs and priorities (U.S. Department of Education, 2016a). The rules also require new reporting by states about program effectiveness that facilitates ongoing feedback among programs, prospective teachers, schools and districts, states and the public (U.S. Department of Education, 2016a).

The regulations specifically provide transparency around the effectiveness of all preparation programs (traditional, alternative routes, and distance) by requiring states to report annually, at the program level, on a variety of factors (U.S. Department of Education, 2016a). States must report on student learning outcomes that are measured by new teacher growth, evaluation results, and other state measures related to student outcomes, including academic performance (U.S. Department of Education, 2016a). In reporting on student learning outcomes, states are able to determine their own relevant measures, some of which may not necessarily be directly tied to student achievement nor educator evaluation results (U.S. Department of Education, 2016a).

States are allowed flexibility in whether or not to report on any additional measures as well as how much weight to give each measure; however, they are required to categorize program effectiveness using at least three levels of performance (effective, at-risk, and low-performing). States are also required to provide technical assistance to any program rated as low-performing to help it improve (U.S. Department of Education, 2016a).

Regulations also provide that states must engage a wide variety of stakeholders and providers to develop and improve meaningful systems meant to identify programs that are effective as well as those that are low-performing (U.S. Department of Education, 2016a). Indicators must be established and used by states to report on teacher preparation program performance and to help ensure that the quality of any given program is determined by reliable and valid indicators (U.S. Department of Education, 2016a).

Benefits of the regulations include improvements to accountability systems that will enable prospective teachers to make better informed choices about enrollment in preparation programs, enable employers of prospective teachers to make better informed hiring decisions, and regulations that create incentives for states to monitor and continuously improve the quality of their teacher preparation programs (U.S. Department of Education, 2016a). Of most importance, the regulations will support students who benefit from better prepared, higher-quality teachers in the classroom, particularly for those in high-need schools and communities or those who are disproportionately taught by less experienced teachers (U.S. Department of Education, 2016a).

P12 PARTNERSHIPS

The P12 teaching profession is consistently having to do more while being provided with less. Growing expectations in conjunction with declining independence for teachers, less pay, constrained budgets, and acute teacher shortages are becoming the standard in certain regions and subject areas (Horvath & Caulfield, 2016). At the same time, teacher preparation programs are experiencing declining enrollment; increased costs; difficulties in recruiting diverse students in critical-needs areas such as special education, math, and science; and withering budgets, all while being the subject of policy-maker and media criticism (Horvath & Caulfield, 2016). In order to combat these issues, it is essential that teacher preparation programs have strong relationships with P12 partners.

Despite evidence that many social factors affect student performance in P12, communities often blame low student outcomes on the quality of teacher preparation programs in higher education. Critics look for improvements in teacher education, including more uniform standards for preparation, teacher performance, and P12 student learning outcomes (Horvath & Caulfield, 2016). Critics would also like to see a more evidence-based approach to teacher training, stricter standards for teacher licensure, more stringent measures of teacher quality, and more rigorous P12 student learning outcomes (Horvath & Caulfield, 2016).

P12 EDUCATOR CHALLENGES

Budget Constraints. When school funding is reduced, the ability of school districts to recruit, hire, and retain high-quality teachers is restricted and layoffs, furloughs, and pay cuts become more common (Horvath & Caulfield, 2016). In particular, under-resourced schools may have the inability to compete with wealthier schools, not only in paying teachers, but also in providing adequate resources to address diverse student needs (Horvath & Caulfield, 2016). As a result of budget constraints, teachers must teach classes with more students, especially in schools located in high-poverty communities. An additional difficulty exists in implementing and maintaining new technology for students and educators alike (Horvath & Caulfield, 2016).

Increased Expectations and Declining Independence. The 21st-century teacher is faced with new responsibilities and under pressure to track and document student progress as well as to understand how the data should be applied to improve teaching and learning within the classroom (Horvath & Caulfield, 2016).

Teachers are expected to master complicated content areas as well as be experts in emerging technologies and pedagogies, such as blended learning (Horn & Staker, 2015). Teachers are consistently expected to know how to effectively teach all students at all academic levels, including students with disabilities, and from different cultural, linguistic, and socioeconomic backgrounds. The new educational norm is for teachers to provide personalized learning, customized class modules, and assignments specifically designed for individual students (Horn & Staker, 2015; Horvath & Caulfield, 2016).

TEACHERS' EVOLVING ROLES WITHIN THE CLASSROOM

Successful and effective teachers are essential to improved student learning, and teacher effectiveness can be developed through preparation programs that purposefully train educators to teach higher standards to students in urban, suburban, and rural classrooms (National Conference of State Legislators, 2013). Educator preparation programs must provide expert instruction to preservice teachers regarding the content areas to be taught, knowledge of learning strategies, and the ability to differentiate instruction based on student need (National Conference of State Legislators, 2013). Preparation programs must also focus on how to use data to identify excelling and struggling students and the skills necessary to use classroom technology to create new paths of access and understanding for every student (National Conference of State Legislators, 2013).

In order for teachers to be deemed effective, they must understand and apply strategies that will help students increase achievement, such as developing a positive classroom environment, as well as stimulating student learning and development. Effective teachers also should understand and apply knowledge of child and adolescent development to not only motivate and engage students, but to recognize and diagnose individual learning needs (National Council for Accreditation of Teacher Education, 2014).

Traditionally, the role of a teacher has been to plan and deliver instruction, help students apply concepts through classroom instruction and presentations, assess student learning, grade papers, manage the classroom, meet with parents, and work collaboratively with school administration and staff (Cox, 2017a; Stronge, Grant, & Xu, 2015a). For 21st-century teachers, the role has manifested itself into much more than just executing lesson plans, it has become a multifaceted profession in which teachers play, at a minimum, the role of surrogate parent, class disciplinarian, mentor, counselor, bookkeeper, role model, and planner (Cox, 2017a). Teachers are also taking on other roles in education such as working with politicians, colleagues, and community members to set clear and obtainable student standards (Cox, 2017a).

Great teachers understand and acknowledge that in order to be effective, they must wear more than one hat to ensure a successful school day, a positive learning environment, and a quality education for all students (Meier, 2018). One of the myriad roles an educator plays is being a learner through consistent professional development classes, learning best practices in the field as well as new strategies for effective teaching. When regular collaboration occurs between teachers, they are able to gain new ideas for teaching, plan grade-level instruction, and combine subjects to enhance the learning experience (Meier, 2018; School Courses & Career Development, 2017).

Teachers are also expected to analyze test results and other data to determine the course of instruction and to determine appropriate changes in the classrooms (Meier, 2018; School Courses & Career Development, 2017). Designing lesson plans and providing students with engaging activities while taking into account each student's interests and instructional needs are also on the to-do list (Meier, 2017; Meier, 2018).

Teaching should not be lecturing, but rather facilitating learning—that is, providing students with the right information, materials, and tools needed to master a subject (Meier, 2018). Teachers often work in a tutoring capacity with individual or small groups of students and are constantly assessing and evaluating students' abilities by way of formal and informal assessments in order to make suggestions for improvement and to assign appropriate grades (School Courses & Career Development, 2017).

One of the most important roles a teacher holds involves interacting with students (Meier, 2018). Teachers are seen as leaders within the classroom and the school who have earned the respect of students by setting a positive example and demonstrating care and concern for not only the students' academic success but their overall well-being (School Courses & Career Development, 2017). By supporting students and having their best interests at heart, teachers often act as counselors and surrogate parents (Meier, 2018).

Teachers must also establish a classroom climate that encourages participation and risk taking so that students are more likely to be involved and engaged in the learning process (Meier, 2017).To ensure a successful classroom environment, teachers must implement structure, develop positive student interaction, and take immediate actions when problems arise (Meier, 2017). When classrooms become out of control, research demonstrates students will perform with lower levels of academic achievement and teachers will have higher rates of stress and exhaustion (Meier, 2017).

Regular classroom instruction also should include teaching an understanding of social skills as well as helping students understand that facing adversity is a natural part of learning. Teachers are also held as disciplinarians, as their role includes handing out just and steady punishments to students who break the rules (School Courses & Career Development, 2017). Discussing consequences for unacceptable behavior has been demonstrated to help students develop critical thinking skills and become better decision makers (Meier, 2017).

BLENDED CLASSROOMS

The use of blended classroom instruction requires teachers to plan curriculum and instruction ahead of time in ways that are different from regular classroom instruction (Horn & Staker, 2015). Instead of developing curriculum on a weekly basis, instructional strategies must be configured in advance and feature the necessary resources for accommodating differentiated instructional strategies as well as assistive elements (Bhagi, 2016). By planning in advance, teachers will have more free time to focus on data analysis and personalize the course for real-time adaptive adjustments based on students' learning paths (Bhagi, 2016).

In a blended classroom, teachers will need to assume the role of classroom manager, setting students up with individual paths but the same learning goals (Horn & Staker, 2015). Students in a blended classroom all work differently, on different content, on different tasks, at a different pace, and in different groups; thus, teachers must set appropriate learning norms and checkpoints, as well as engage all learners with differentiated tactics (Bhagi, 2016). Teachers must make the shift from teacher-centric classroom styles toward the role of a guide on the side who can effectively manage students at different learning abilities, deliver quality instructions, and proactively troubleshoot student limitations (Bhagi, 2016).

Teachers in blended learning classrooms also collect data on student performance to analyze content engagement and offer adaptive and personalized learning (Horn & Staker, 2015). Proactive analyzation of student performance data will allow teachers to keep track of individual learning and monitor each student's struggles and gaps in the content and curriculum, as well as their successes (Bhagi, 2016). Instructing a blended learning classroom requires teachers to transform learning materials into more engaging content, such as video tutorials, learning through doing, eBooks, online lectures, and podcasts, in order to engage all learning styles and abilities (Bhagi, 2016).

21ST-CENTURY TEACHING

The goals of the 21st-century teacher should be the development of knowledge, character, and the higher-order skills of creativity, critical thinking, communication, and collaboration (Stronge et al., 2015a). Becoming an effective teacher should also include the establishment of lifelong learning habits and an ability to learn how to learn with technology (Stronge et al., 2015a). Designing technology-integrated learning is crucial in effective teaching. A teacher's confidence, attitude toward technology integration, and willingness to incorporate technology use for student learning are indicative of a great 21st century teacher (Stronge et al., 2015a).

The role of the 21st-century teacher includes teachers as planners for future, not-yet-developed careers. Stronge et al. (2015a) predict that there will be greater diversity and autonomy for students to choose what and how to learn and that their potential may be in areas that are beyond the core standards; thus, teachers must incorporate new ways of knowing grounded in technology. Effective teachers should plan lessons that give priority to the skills students can carry across disciplines and into new and different employment opportunities. Thinking, problem solving, collaboration, and communication should be at the forefront, providing the means for all students to navigate multi-disciplinary landscapes (Stronge et al., 2015b).

In planning instruction, teachers must remember that to remain effective, they need to give up the notion that they are only content experts; they need to plan to be facilitators who provide the scaffolding to support students in the development of their own personal ways of knowing and thinking (Stronge et al., 2015a). Instead of using uniform strategies for all students, teachers must design instruction that motivates each student by providing experiential, authentic, and challenging experiences while still communicating content in ways that students are able to comprehend based on their individual learning and ability (Stronge et al., 2015a).

Implementing various classroom strategies will also enhance student motivation and decrease disciplinary problems, while differentiated instruction enables teachers to adjust their curriculum, materials, learning activities, and assessment techniques. These measures ensure that all students in a mixed classroom have opportunities to process new knowledge and develop skills while having equal access to high-quality learning (Stronge et al., 2015b).

Scaffolded implementation of content provides incentives for students to take an active and participative role in their own learning (Stronge et al., 2015a). Students are prompted to manage their own learning as the teacher provides examples, explanations and feedback. Effective instruction can also take place when the teacher anchors learning activities to real-life problems that students can identify with while modeling the thinking process or procedures needed to solve problems and perform unfamiliar tasks (Stronge, et al., 2015a).

One of the most powerful ways to increase student learning is to make instruction relevant to the students. Relevancy allows students to explore, inquire, and meaningfully construct knowledge of real problems that are relevant to their lives, while offering motivating and engaging learning. Authentic and real-world tasks that are deeply examined show the greatest personalized results (Stronge, et al., 2015b).

TEACHERS AS LEADERS

For quite some time teachers have served as team leaders, department chairs, association leaders, and curriculum developers, and in these roles, they have been more like representatives than leaders (Boyd-Dimock & McGee, 2017). Traditionally, teacher leadership roles have lacked flexibility and required a lengthy, ongoing commitment of time and energy where teachers give up their teaching role and make the switch into administration (Boyd-Dimock & McGee, 2017).

Recently, there has been a great deal of advocacy for teachers to expand their roles into leadership positions, as they have daily contact with students. The belief is that educators are in the most advantageous position to make critical decisions about curriculum and instruction and are better able to implement changes in a comprehensive and continuous manner (Boyd-Dimock & McGee, 2017). Transitioning into leadership roles is grounded in the desire of teachers to improve the quality of teaching and learning for all students and is seen as a collaborative effort to promote professional development and growth and the improvement of educational services (Boyd-Dimock & McGee, 2017).

As we move further into the 21st century, new leadership roles are emerging and providing real opportunities for teachers to impact educational change without leaving the classroom. Teachers are serving in new roles such as research colleagues, advisor-mentors, facilitators of professional development activities, members of school-based leadership teams, instructional support teams, and leaders of change efforts (Boyd-Dimock & McGee, 2017).

In order to be effective with their colleagues, teacher leaders must learn a variety of leadership skills including building trust and developing rapport, diagnosing organizational conditions, dealing with processes, managing the work, and building skills and confidence in others (Boyd-Dimock & McGee, 2017). Teacher-leaders must also model collegiality, enhance teachers' self-esteem, and encourage others to provide leadership to their peers (Boyd-Dimock & McGee, 2017).

As a result of their involvement in leadership positions, teachers will see a direct correlation between an increase in their knowledge and skills and greater confidence and a stronger commitment to teaching. Observation, assistance to other teachers, and working with administrators will expose teachers to new concepts and ideas, leading to a significant amount of professional growth (Boyd-Dimock & McGee, 2017). Teacher leaders, in addition, will experience a significant decrease in isolation as a result of increased opportunities to work with others (Boyd-Dimock and McGee, 2017).

FINAL THOUGHTS

Well-prepared teachers will produce higher student achievement, generate more student earning potential, and remain in the teaching profession longer. In order to have well-prepared and effective new teachers, the Department of Education has made revisions to its teacher preparation program regulations. Prospective teachers are now able to make informed choices about enrollment in teacher preparation programs and employers are better informed regarding hiring new educators. These new and revised regulations are also designed to ensure that inexperienced teachers are ready to succeed in the classroom and that all students are taught by well-prepared educators. Most importantly, the regulations support student success through high-quality teachers in the classroom (Stronge et al., 2015b).

Teachers now hold multifaceted roles in which they do more than just plan lessons and lecture. At a minimum, educators must play the role of surrogate parent, class disciplinarian, mentor, counselor, bookkeeper, role model, and planner. Uniform strategies of the past are no longer enough, and instruction designed to motivate each student must include experiential, authentic, and challenging experiences while communicating content in comprehensive ways based on individual learning and ability.

Implementing various classroom strategies will enhance student motivation and allow teachers to adjust their curriculum, materials, learning activities, and assessment techniques. Combined, these strategies ensure that all students have access to high-quality learning and opportunities to process new knowledge and develop skills.

POINTS TO REMEMBER

- Regulations for preservice programs provide transparency surrounding the effectiveness of all training, as states must report student learning outcomes as measured by new teacher growth, evaluation results, and academic performance of students. States can now determine their own student learning outcome measures unrelated to student achievement.
- Effective teachers must understand and apply strategies to help increase student achievement and stimulate student learning. Effective teachers should also understand and apply knowledge regarding child development so as to motivate and engage students as well as recognize and diagnose individual learning needs.
- Teachers of blended classrooms should plan curriculum and instruction in advance with the necessary resources for accommodating differentiated instructional strategies, leaving them more time to analyze data and personalize their students' learning paths.
- Proactive analyzation of student performance data allows teachers to track the learning pace of each student and individually monitor his or her struggles as well as reveal gaps in the content and curriculum.
- Goals of the 21st-century teacher include the development of knowledge, character, and higher-order skills such as creativity, critical thinking, communication, and collaboration. Effective teaching should also establish lifelong learning habits and the ability to use technology—integrated as a crucial tool toward effective teaching.
- The most powerful way to increase student learning is to make instruction relevant to the students, which, in turn, produces personalized results. Students are then more willing to explore, inquire, and meaningfully construct knowledge of real problems.

Chapter Two

Collaboration Is Key

Embracing Meaningful Teamwork

Collaborative practices have increased significantly over the past few decades in part due to the inclusion of students with disabilities, the increase in English-language learners, and the implementation of the Common Core State Standards (Welborn, 2012). Currently, classrooms contain a diverse set of students that requires knowledgeable teachers to meet their needs. One way this can be accomplished is through effective collaboration (Burton, 2015; Green & Allen, 2015; Watson, 2014; Welborn, 2012).

Collaboration is a systematic approach for analyzing the art of teaching and learning (Burton, 2015). Through collaborative efforts, the needs of diverse student populations can be met, teacher efficacy can be increased, and enhanced learning opportunities are possible (Welborn, 2012). An important finding in the literature suggests that all teachers benefit from collaboration despite the level of individual contributions to the group (Burton, 2015).

Research has shown that collaboration between teachers produces both individual and collective benefits (Welborn, 2012). Collaboration should be focused, sustained, perceived as helpful, and productive in nature in order to increase both student achievement and teacher performance (Burton, 2015). These findings align with suggestions set forth by Welborn (2012), who concluded that effective collaborative efforts must have a clearly defined purpose, require individual commitment, have an understanding of how to collaborate, receive support from administration, and support the individual freedom to explore.

Burton (2015) identified five components to effective collaboration, including having defined roles and responsibilities, a shared vision, aligning efforts to the culture of the school, developing a collaborative strategic plan, and having the opportunity to assess and adjust the plan. These components work in harmony together to support any cooperative activity; however, there are also three major challenges to collaborative efforts including inconsistency; lack of resources, including time; and diverse personalities and beliefs (Burton, 2015).

Learning Forward (2017) developed professional learning standards to support collaborative efforts and focus on supporting teaching and learning. The standards further outline the necessary supports to encourage the development of knowledge, skills, practices, and dispositions of teachers that promote student performance (Learning Forward, 2017).

The 2012 MET Life teacher survey indicated that only 6 out of 10 teachers felt that they had time to participate in collaborative activities (Vislocky, 2013). With the adoption of the common core standards, however, cooperative efforts are at the heart of any hope to raise student achievement scores. According to Vislocky (2013), effective collaboration occurs through both structured activities as well as through informal teacher-to-teacher interactions.

Watson (2014) examined the effectiveness of professional learning communities (PLCs) as a means of collaboration and found that PLCs work to support student learning through teacher growth. The research described three overarching themes and five smaller components (Watson, 2014). Understanding the research studies more deeply provides opportunities to expand educator learning.

THE GROWTH OF COLLABORATIVE PRACTICES

The collaborative movement dates back to the mid-1970s with the initial enactment of the Education of All Handicapped Children Act of 1975, now known as the Individuals with Disabilities Education Improvement Act of 2004 (IDEA) (National Center for Learning Disabilities, 2006; American Psychological Association, 2017). The original intent of the act was to marry special education and general education teachers in a collaborative partnership as a way to educate students with disabilities (Burton 2015). Since that time, inclusion debates have kept the idea of collaboration at the forefront of best educational practices.

Through collaborative efforts to address the needs of diverse student populations, teachers build efficacy, improve attitudes, and gain a better understanding of the various learning profiles of different student populations (Burton 2015; Green & Allen, 2015). Both students and teachers reap the benefits of cooperative efforts including developing greater skill variety, enhanced learning opportunities, and increased content knowledge and pedagogy (Burton, 2015; Green & Allen, 2015).

ESSENTIAL COMPONENTS OF COLLABORATIVE EFFORTS

Collaboration is more than just a group of individuals working together. In order for collaborative efforts to be beneficial, the literature highlights several essential components including clarity of purpose, individual commitment, collaborative time, understanding the process of working in the partnership, a greater commitment in terms of administrative support, and the freedom to explore learning more deeply (Geeraerts et al., 2015; Welborn, 2012). A closer examination of the six components reveals the interconnections between them.

Clarity of purpose looks to identify a common reason why all individuals are participating in the activity and identify strategies to reach an agreed-upon outcome of the cooperative effort (Welborn, 2012). The collaborative time component identifies ways to structure activities so they can be beneficial and productive, thus, eliminating wasted time and encouraging greater opportunities (Welborn, 2012).

Understanding how to collaborate and communicate efficiently is another component essential to cooperative learning. Standards for professional learning have been developed to provide support for individuals engaged in collaboration. These standards identify the need for active listening and setting group norms (Learning Forward, 2017; Welborn, 2012). Administrative support should focus on creating meaningful collaborative activities, and encouraging teacher autonomy (Welborn, 2012).

The freedom to explore and choose professional learning opportunities is important as educator needs vary based on a variety of reasons. School leaders should embrace the idea that teachers have individual ways in which they would like to collaborate and engage in professional learning (Welborn, 2012). Some teachers may like participating in professional learning communities within their schools, while others may prefer to engage in learning opportunities in alternate locations and with other, similarly minded educators.

FORMS OF COLLABORATION

According to Burton (2015), collaboration is a systematic approach for analyzing and improving instruction and student outcomes. Through collaboration, teachers share experiences, gain knowledge, have a voice, and feel a sense of community and support. Collaboration can come in many forms, including, but not limited to, department teams, grade-level teams, vertical grade teams, student support teams, instructional leadership teams, and cooperative teaching approaches (Burton, 2015).

Regardless of the collaboration type, there are several components necessary for ensuring effectiveness, which include the alignment of school culture, defined roles and responsibilities, establishment of a shared vision, creation of a collaborative strategic plan, and opportunities to assess and adjust said plan (Burton, 2015).

COLLABORATION AND PROFESSIONAL LEARNING

Collaboration embraces the idea of shared accountability and individual growth and is often the primary vehicle for continuous improvement in teacher performance (Green & Allen, 2015). Research has shown that sustained collaborative activities among teachers boosts student achievement, increases teacher effectiveness, and supports nurturing and respectful learning environments (Green & Allen, 2015; Learning Forward, 2017).

Learning Forward (2017) identified three overarching themes that result from collaborative efforts, including collective responsibility, continuous improvement, and shared accountability. The same organization developed six focus standard areas to support professional learning, including leadership, resources, data, learning design, implementation, and outcomes (Learning Forward, 2017).

The leadership standard examines the role of the school leader in the collaboration process (Learning Forward, 2017; Green & Allen, 2015). Effective school leaders should be advocates of professional learning and provide the structure and support needed to carry our collaborative efforts. Through the school leader, teachers can develop the capacity to grow professionally. The resources standard simply acknowledges the assets required for successful collaboration to occur, those of time, staff, and materials (Learning Forward, 2017).

The appropriate use of educator, student, and district data encompasses the data standard and it identifies ways to plan, monitor, and evaluate the impact of professional learning opportunities (Green & Allen, 2015). The learning design standard highlights the benefits of active engagement combined with ideas from social interaction theories to support the critical need for cooperative learning experiences (Learning Forward, 2017).

Within the implementation standard, the association acknowledges the need for sustained support by all stakeholders and the benefit of corrective feedback throughout the process (Learning Forward, 2017). These ideas and recognitions are grounded in the research on application of change (Green & Allen, 2015). The outcomes standard identifies the coherence between what students learn, what teachers learn, and the goals of the school and school system and stresses the importance of aligning teacher performance with student outcomes (Learning Forward, 2017).

PROFESSIONAL LEARNING COMMUNITIES

The goal of any professional learning community (PLC) is to consistently engage educational professionals in the learning process for the benefit of students (Gore et al., 2017; Watson, 2014). The ultimate focus of PLCs is to support student learning opportunities. Through research, Watson (2014) concluded there were three overarching themes that must be present and supported within professional learning communities for them to be successful: shared values and vision, a focus on learning, and a sense of community.

Under the theme of shared values and visions, organization of the learning community should be evident in the policies and practices of the school and/or district (Watson, 2014). Shared values and visions must be articulated clearly so that all involved know the vision and purpose of the collaborative efforts. The focus on learning premise asserts that the learning acquired by educators should be content focused, strategy focused, coherent, and occurring during the collaborative activities through collective participation (Watson, 2014). A sense of community ensures that everyone has a feeling of belonging within an atmosphere of mutual trust (Gore et al., 2017; Watson, 2014).

In addition to the three overarching themes, Watson (2014) identified eight key characteristics of professional learning communities, which can be separated into two interconnected categories: learning within the PLC and the notion of community. Within the theme of learning within the PLC, five characteristics are supported. When individuals engage in collaborative learning efforts, they must agree upon the vision of the work they are doing. The values established set the tone of the community and determine whether the team will be successful or not (Watson, 2014).

The second characteristic points out the importance of collective responsibility for student learning (Watson, 2014). Again, the idea that professional learning communities have the capacity to promote and sustain teacher learning to increase student achievement suggests that it is a team effort. The third component, reflective professional inquiry, supports the idea that regular engagement in reflective practices encourages academic growth (Watson, 2014).

Learning-focused collaboration ensures members continuously strive for the intended outcome—that of increasing student achievement and professional growth for educators (Gore et al., 2017; Watson, 2014). The last characteristic under the first theme promotes the idea that the group, as well as its individual members, must be learning (Watson, 2014). As the ultimate goal of professional learning communities is increasing student achievement, when educators are collaborating together to identify ways to help their students, they too are increasing their knowledge in the form of content-related or pedagogical skills (Watson, 2014).

CHALLENGES TO EFFECTIVE COLLABORATION

The benefits of collaboration are plenty; however, the literature has identified several aspects that have been shown to present challenges. Inconsistency is highlighted throughout the research as a frequent roadblock to collaboration (Burton, 2015). Similar to rituals and routines in the classroom, collaboration activities need to occur consistently so that they become a regular and expected facet of teaching and learning (Burton, 2015). In order to overcome inconsistency, school administrators should schedule regular collaborative activities with staff and provide structured action plans as well as required outcomes.

Collaborative efforts involve individuals working together and, as such, the likelihood of there being diverse personalities and beliefs, thus sometimes presenting challenges (Burton, 2015). One way to address this is to have clearly delineated rules for any and all collaborative activities. Rules should include such things as active listening, showing respect for other viewpoints, and identifying ways to overcome various viewpoints as well a team-appointed leader to moderate cooperative efforts within the group (Burton, 2015).

Other challenges often faced by teachers are a lack of resources and time and the pressure to produce results from collaborative efforts (Burton, 2015). School administrators need to be aware that in order to produce results through collaboration, teachers need time and resources to fully engage in the professional learning process. Administrators can factor these needs into their budgeting plans, as well as their scheduling opportunities.

FINAL THOUGHTS

With today's diverse student population in our inclusive classrooms, the need for teacher collaboration is not only beneficial but critical as well (Burton, 2015; Watson, 2014; Welborn, 2012). Through collaborative efforts that enhance learning opportunities, all students' needs can be met (Welborn, 2012). Consistent and structured collaboration between teachers has been proven to increase student achievement and enhance teacher performance (Burton, 2015). When collaboration is focused, supported, and aligned, students reap the benefits of increased engagement and learning opportunities.

When engaging in collaborative efforts, it is important to have defined roles and responsibilities, create a shared vision, align group efforts to the school's vision, develop a strategic plan, and assess the plan consistently (Burton, 2015). Best practices in collaborative professional learning center around the three overarching themes of collective responsibility, continuous improvement, and shared accountability, and related focus standards provide resources and support for each criterion (Learning Forward, 2017).

Professional learning communities are one form of cooperative learning that works to support student learning through teacher growth. Three important themes have emerged, including having shared values and visions, a focus on learning, and a sense of community (Watson, 2014). Within these three themes, smaller components were discovered; they include collective responsibility for student learning, reflective professional inquiry, collective activities for learning, and ensuring that all members must be learning (Watson, 2014).

POINTS TO REMEMBER

- Collaboration is considered a systematic approach for improving teaching and learning efforts. It is through collaboration that learning opportunities are enhanced and teacher efficacy increases.
- For collaborative efforts to be beneficial, they must be focused, sustained, perceived as helpful, and productive. They must also be clearly defined, have individual commitment, receive administrative support, and encourage the freedom to explore a variety of possibilities.
- Specific components must be present for collaborative efforts to be beneficial, including defining roles and responsibilities, having a shared vision, aligning efforts to the culture of the school, developing a strategic plan, and assessing and revising the plan as needed.
- Three major challenges to collaborative efforts include inconsistency; lack of resources, including time; and diverse personalities and beliefs. In order to compensate for these challenges, schools are encouraged to schedule regular collaborative activities, develop rules and rituals for engaging in collaborative efforts, and budget for future cooperative endeavors.

Chapter Three

The Home-School Connection

Promoting and Sustaining Successful Partnerships

Positive and healthy relationships between teachers and students are extremely valuable to the student, the classroom, and the entire school environment. There are a variety of benefits that can be gained from establishing positive student-teacher relationships, ranging from improved self-esteem to increased engagement (Pride Surveys, 2016a). As positive student-teacher relationships develop over time, enduring effects benefit not only teachers and students but teachers and parents as well.

Strong relationships between teacher/student, teacher/family, and family/school provide some of the most important factors in the academic success of students and are significantly influential on student success and growth both in and out of the classroom (Richert, 2017; SimplyCircle, 2015; Magsamen, 2015; Starr, 2017). Families can be significant resources, and taking the time to collaborate with families will make teaching easier and increase students' chances for success (Richert, 2017).

Successful first-year teachers say parental involvement in education, both at home and in the classroom, is vital to effective learning and discipline (Hare, 2017). When parents know what is happening in the classroom and at school, they are better able to partner with teachers to enhance and support student success (Simply Circle, 2015). Children benefit from guidance by their parents in all settings; thus, parental attitudes about education will significantly affect how children perform (Gaunt, 2017).

Positive relationships help parents understand their student's unique strengths, interests, and talents as learning patterns emerge (Magsamen, 2015). Relationships take time to build; however, in most cases, teachers change every year. This makes constant communication, collaboration, creative problem solving, common goals, and trust essential (Magsamen, 2015). As parents remain a constant factor in a student's education, it is important that they develop leadership skills, have meaningful and productive conversations, and create goals and action plans for supporting their student (Magsamen, 2015).

CREATING FAMILY PARTNERSHIPS

The key to successful parent-teacher collaboration is to become a team and involve parents in student learning (Pride Surveys, 2016b; Starr, 2017). This collaboration is the most powerful tool in helping a child be successful at school and for creating an environment that supports the success of all students (Pride Surveys, 2016b).

To form collaborative and effective partnerships with families, teachers must understand the needs of parents and the community and then establish themselves as a friendly addition to the existing dynamics (Diggs, 2015). Teachers should let go of any judgments and/or preconceptions about families, as respectful alliances can only be formed when the best interests of the student are kept at the forefront (Richter, 2017).

The most important step a teacher can take is to establish his or her availability and willingness to work with parents to help their child succeed (Pride Surveys, 2016b). At the beginning of each school year, teachers should set a positive, welcoming, and inviting tone by making contact with families to introduce themselves (Richert, 2017; Starr, 2017). Teachers should inform parents that they are available to discuss any questions or concerns via phone, text, or email between certain hours or during weekly office hours where parents can schedule in-person appointments (Pride Surveys, 2016b; Starr, 2017).

Teachers should consider sharing how important parent contributions are and the desire to partner with them (Richter, 2017). Good rapport with the family should be built from the outset, before any problems occur, so that the first meeting with a parent is not about negative academic or behavioral performance (Richert, 2017; Hare, 2017; Thompson, 2017). Research has shown that calling parents with good news about their student helps strengthen the teacher-parent relationship (Hare, 2017; Thompson, 2017).

Through supportive communication and collaboration, teachers are also able to assist families with parenting skills, family support, understanding adolescent development, and setting home conditions to support learning (Pride Surveys, 2016b). Information can be disseminated to families on how to create positive learning environments, schedule time for homework, set limits on electronics, and plan to check in with the student about his or her school experiences (Richert, 2017).

Teachers and schools should consider creating a parent resource center that provides materials on issues of concern to parents, such as child development, health and safety, drug education, and special education. Information about local parenting and social services agencies along with sample textbooks, extension activities, software, and audio and videotapes should be made available when possible (Starr, 2017).

Effective partnerships can be sustained through frequent personal communication regarding student needs and classroom activities via emails, newsletters, phone calls, meetings in the classroom, and home visits (Richert, 2017; Hare, 2017; Diggs, 2015). Communications can center on topics such as the family's expectations for the student, how parents can support their student with homework, and how teachers can assist the family (Richert, 2017). Teachers should also inquire if there are any hardships that parents would like to share that may be affecting the student emotionally and if there are any other responsibilities that the student has in addition to school (Richert, 2017).

Two-way communication between teachers and parents is essential (SimplyCircle, 2015; Dunham, 2016; ProSolutions Training, 2015; Diggs, 2015). Teachers are experts, and, as such, they should share their academic expertise with parents as well as listen to the parents' expertise about their own child and the family environment. This give and take helps create a positive atmosphere where both parties can brainstorm together to find the best strategy to support the student (Richter, 2017). It is important that teachers get to know the strengths, weaknesses, fears, and quirks of every student and be able to talk openly with the parents. It may be useful to keep a notebook for each student that includes notes on conversations, interactions, and observations (Sarnofsky, 2016).

Parents can often offer a different perspective, creative ideas, and positive or negative feedback to assist the teacher in understanding the student (SimplyCircle, 2015). Teachers should not be the only ones to ask questions; rather, parents should be encouraged to ask questions about their student and how the classroom is run. In this way, teachers, parents, and even the student, can cocreate goals, and problem solve when necessary. Rewards can be devised for student improvement in addition to consequences for failure to improve (Richert, 2017).

When developing family partnerships, teachers should recognize that family members have various educational backgrounds and may not know how to participate in their student's education. Families are often from different cultural or linguistic backgrounds and may feel alienated from school processes (Richert, 2017). Family dynamics, such as work schedules and transportation, can also influence a parent's ability to participate consistently. Collaboration should account for varying family constraints while problem solving for solutions (Richert, 2017).

Chapter 3
INVOLVING PARENTS

To begin enlisting parents in the process and gaining parental trust, teachers should send home a positive and cheerful letter to introduce themselves that includes their background, class rules and expectations, a description of homework that will be assigned, and grading policies (Thompson, 2017; Cox, 2017a). Contact information such as school phone numbers, teacher's email address, school calendar, and a community services directory should also be included in the letter (Thompson, 2017; Ohio Department of Education, 2016).

Some teachers may want to follow the AIDET model in their initial form of communication, whether it be on the phone, email, website, or in person (Studer Group, 2018). Although this model began as a medical introduction for patients, it is a complete framework for engaging families. Teachers should "Acknowledge" the parent via some form of greeting; it can be as simple as hello. An "Introduction" should follow that outlines the teacher's credentials and training along with an explanation of why they are qualified to teach the student.

Next, teachers should describe the "Duration" and essence of what will occur in the first few weeks of school and/or identify a particular project that the student will be working on. "Explanations" should be included on what will be provided to students and what the expectations will be for the class as a whole and students in particular. Finally, teachers should extend a "Thank-You" to the parents, provide their contact information, and encourage parents to reach out at any time during the school year (Studer Group, 2018; Cox, 2017a).

At the beginning of each school year, schools usually hold an open house where families can meet their student's teachers, tour the school building, and meet other parents. Translators should be in attendance to welcome and assist families at the open house and throughout the school year during activities (Ohio Department of Education, 2016). Teacher-parent interviews and conferences provide a great opportunity to communicate with the students' parents and hear how the students are doing at home both academically and socially relative to their classmates. Interviews can also be used to discuss any troubles or questions either person has regarding the student as well as develop strategies, goals, and plans for the students' future (ProSolutions Training, 2015; Pride Surveys, 2016b; Starr, 2017).

Concerns, questions, and comments can be outlined ahead of time to make the most out of the allotted time (ProSolutions Training, 2015). Parents who cannot attend conferences should still be given the opportunity to speak with the teacher by phone or email to become familiar with the teachers' goals, structure of the class, and the student's progress (Gaunt, 2017).

Teachers should work toward building an "emotional bank account" with parents by way of sincere, positive, and clear communication, as well as efforts to demonstrate that both the students and parents matter (Cox, 2017b). To ensure parents feel valued and that their opinion is appreciated, teachers should consider asking the following questions: What do you think is helping your student the most in making sure he or she hits his or her learning targets? Do you see any gaps keeping your student from hitting his or her targets? and Do you believe your student has all the information he or she needs to hit the targets? (Cox, 2017b).

Some parents may become over-involved and end up being a source of distraction for the student, their classmates, and/or teacher. Parents should be reminded that school is not only a place of learning but a workplace as well and that loud conversations, particularly about teachers and students, are not acceptable (Gaunt, 2017). Teachers that have students in class that may become easily distracted, lose focus, or encounter behavior issues with a parent in the room, should inform them that they may still be involved in volunteer opportunities that can take place outside the classroom (Gaunt, 2017).

Teachers will also be able to invite parents into the classroom where the teacher can present a PowerPoint with slides on who they are, including family, education, and experience, as well as contact information and the school's website. An explanation of what the class will work on, rules and regulations, and expectations should also be highlighted during this event (Williams, 2017; Ohio Department of Education, 2016). Teachers are encouraged to hold parent activities, such as coffee and conversation hours or breakfasts, that introduce all the elements of the school's culture (Sarnovsky, 2016).

If the school does not already do it, teachers should consider sending home a student information sheet that requests basic information such as student's and parent's names, address, phone numbers, and email addresses (Williams, 2017). A call home during the beginning of the school year can also be made as a way to learn about the students; asking parents questions to elicit information on what they should know about a student and what has worked well in school for them in the past helps create a bond that will pay off later in the year (Thompson, 2017).

Class websites may be set up listing a short biography of the teacher, contact information, grading system, tutoring after school, and expectations/goals (Williams, 2017). Websites are also a great place to create a suggestion or comment box for parents to anonymously provide their questions, concerns and recommendations (Ohio Department of Education, 2016; Starr, 2017).

Parents can also easily access information on upcoming events, assignments, field trips, and volunteer opportunities that provide meaningful work and flexible scheduling (Thompson, 2017; Pride Surveys, 2016b; Starr, 2017).

Surveys can be distributed to parents to identify volunteer interests, talents and availability in order to match parental interests to school programs and staff-support needs (Ohio Department of Education, 2016). Parents may not be proactive in reaching out to teachers and are more likely to volunteer when a teacher requests help within the classroom or at the student's home. Teachers can involve families in reading groups, remedial assistance, or classroom tasks (Hare, 2017; SimplyCircle, 2015). Parents may also be invited into the classroom to present talks and/or demonstrations about their specialized knowledge or skills (Starr, 2017).

Teachers should help families to be involved with their student in learning at home, including homework, goal setting, and other curriculum-related activities (Gaunt, 2017; Pride Surveys, 2016b; Ohio Department of Education, 2016). Teachers should inform parents of how they can reinforce classroom learning within the home environment and may want to ask them to sign a contract with their student to reinforce the importance of completing homework and other home learning activities (Hare, 2017; Ohio Department of Education, 2016; Starr, 2017).

Although there is a strong push for parental involvement through parent-teacher associations, some parents may feel alienated if they cannot be involved due to work schedules or other circumstances. Schools should let parents know that coming in during the school day is not the only way that parents help (Gaunt, 2017). One way that teachers can help parents feel involved is by compiling a wish list that includes both classroom necessities and extra items, anything from tissues and antibacterial wipes to craft sticks and carpet squares. Teachers should make sure that there is something on there for every parent by including free or inexpensive items (Starr, 2017).

Families should also be included as participants in school decisions, governance, and advocacy activities through school councils or improvement teams, committees, and other organizations. Teachers and schools should create roles for parents on decision-making and advisory committees as well as train parents to serve in their chosen role (Ohio Department of Education, 2016). By establishing policies and procedures that address the above initiatives, schools can begin establishing a school-wide community and culture that promotes positive parent-teacher cooperation and communication.

Teachers and parents should partner with local agencies to provide regular parenting workshops and materials on child development, appropriate parent and school expectations, nutrition, family recreation and/or communication (Ohio Department of Education, 2016; Starr, 2017). A list of community resources such as summer programs and activities may be disseminated to parents that link student learning skills and talents (Ohio Department of Education, 2016; Starr, 2017).

School-business partnerships may also be established to provide student mentoring programs, internships, and onsite, experiential learning opportunities as well as service-learning projects in the community. In turn, community partners should be invited to open-houses and other school activities to share resources (Ohio Department of Education, 2016).

It is beneficial if the teacher sends home a weekly folder to the parent of every child in the classroom that contains the work for the week, a classroom newsletter and other important documents. Another helpful tool is an electronic grading system so parents are able to monitor their student's progress (Ohio Department of Education, 2016).

When frustrated or upset with a student or classroom situation, teachers should not call home and dump the problem onto the parents. Instead, teachers should employ the "three call method" to establish a positive, working relationship with parents (Pride Surveys, 2016b). Near the beginning of the school year, teachers should try to call each student's parents to set the framework for a partnership. The second time the teacher calls home it should focus on something positive, such as a good grade or excellent behavior. By using this method, teachers will already have an established, trusting, and workable relationship in the event a third call is necessary to discuss any issues or problems that have come up in class (Pride Surveys, 2016b).

Any parental concerns should be addressed head on, in a timely manner, and without educational jargon, particularly if the teacher's approach is pedagogical in nature (Hare, 2017; Starr, 2017). Discussing the benefits of, and reasoning behind, the teacher's approach will help parents understand expectations for student achievement and behavior (Hare, 2017). In meetings, time should be left for parents to ask questions and receive appropriate and thorough answers. If the answer to a question is not known, teachers should promise to call with the answer as soon as possible (Hare, 2017; Starr, 2017).

It is essential that teachers document every conversation that they have with parents. Documentation should include the date, parent/student name, and a brief summary of the conversation. Parents may not remember every conversation so it is extremely useful to have a record to show that you did indeed speak with them (Williams, 2017). A parent might claim that the teacher did not discuss the student's learning challenges that have been noted in class; however, if the teacher has documented the conversation, then the parents will have no basis for their claim (Williams, 2017).

Teachers will not always get along with every child's parent, due to personality conflicts and dissimilar interests. Although there may be some discord, teachers have a job to perform and avoiding parents would not put the student first (Williams, 2017). If teachers try hard enough, they should be able to form some sort of positive relationship and find common ground with the parent that will benefit the student (Williams, 2017).

BENEFITS OF TEACHER-PARENT PARTNERSHIPS

Teachers are the most likely people to understand the impact a students' home life has on the school day. Established teacher-parent relationships built on strong cooperation and communication will increase student success both inside and outside the classroom (Pride Surveys, 2016b). A student who is aware that his or her teacher is in regular communication with a parent and knows that there is trust between the adults in his or her life, will generally put more effort into school (Meador, 2017a). Similarly, a student who knows that the teacher barely, if ever, communicates with parents will often set the two against each other (Meador, 2017a).

Parent involvement has always been, and continues to be, a strong predictor of academic achievement from kindergarten through high school, resulting in fewer grade retentions and higher graduation rates (Pride Surveys, 2016b). Strong relationships between teachers and families, resulting in an increase in family involvement in education, has been linked to improved grades and test scores, as well as improved student behavior, higher self-esteem, and better school attendance (Richert, 2017; SimplyCircle, 2015; Gaunt, 2017; Starr, 2017). When parents are informed and involved in the classroom or at the school, students have higher self-confidence and feel more supported in their learning efforts (SimplyCircle, 2015).

Students also benefit when parents and teachers work together and have open and effective lines of communication by feeling more comforted and confident (ProSolutions, 2015; Pride Surveys, 2016b). Strong teacher-parent relationships are especially critical when younger students start becoming more independent (ProSolutions Training, 2015). Parents who have good relationships with teachers are also in a better place to help their student. Introducing routines and modeling specific behavior at home allows parents to create continuity between expectations at school and home, increasing the likelihood of student success (ProSolutions Training, 2015).

Teachers who establish strong relationships with parents will have better insight into the student's life at home, allowing them to modify individual classroom learning to enhance success (ProSolutions Training, 2015; Dunham, 2016). Parents are experts on their students and, as such, they know what stimulates, bores, and interests them; what they are good at and what they struggle with; what their learning style is; and what issues may affect their learning (Dunham, 2016). To maintain these strong relationships with parents, it is important that teachers reach out early and often, to ask for parental input, particularly before any problems occur.

Parental involvement at school helps build positive interactions between parents and students as well as parents and teachers (Gaunt, 2017). As a result, parents gain a better understanding of their student's school day, which may then improve family communication. Teachers are able to get a better understanding of individual family dynamics, cultural backgrounds, and the strengths and challenges of each family and, in turn, parents can develop a better understanding of the teacher's expectations and the challenges of classroom dynamics (Gaunt, 2017).

FINAL THOUGHTS

Strong relationships between teachers and families result in an increase in family involvement in education and is significantly linked to improved grades and test scores, as well as improved student behavior, more student engagement, higher self-esteem, better school attendance, and academic success. Making a connection with the family is the most important step a teacher can take as it establishes a strong and trustworthy relationship. Parents are then more willing to work with the teacher as a way to help their child succeed.

Although there are many ways for families to be included in school, such as volunteering and sending in wish list items, parents should be involved in school decisions and invited to participate on school councils, advisory committees, or improvement teams. Establishing a school-wide community and culture that promotes positive parent-teacher cooperation and communication will help encourage and further student success.

Although parent involvement decreases as a student gets older, the need for family involvement remains consistent. Students still need parental guidance and encouragement to maintain good habits, manage heavier amounts of homework, and set goals for the future (Richter, 2017).

POINTS TO REMEMBER

- Parental involvement in education, whether it be in the classroom or at home, and parental attitudes toward education in general, are vital to effective learning, discipline, and student success. Successful parent-teacher collaboration requires teamwork and is the most powerful tool to help a child succeed at school.
- Strong relationships between teachers and parents is the strongest predictor of academic achievement and results in improved grades and test scores, better student behavior, higher self-esteem, increased school attendance, and students feeling more supported in their learning efforts.
- Two-way communication between teachers and parents is essential; both are experts and should share their expertise on the student as well as the learning and home environment.

Chapter Four

Positive Classroom Management

Establishing Beneficial Expectations and Norms

Classroom management is comprised of setting expectations, through the use of routines and rituals, in order to create and maintain an organized learning environment that supports teaching and learning (Ministry of Education, 2015). When effective classroom management is in place, it supports academic and social behaviors and appropriate engagement can occur (Emmer & Sabornie, 2015).

Several studies show that there are five components of effective classroom management (Emmer & Sabornie, 2015; Martin et al., 2016). The components include teacher emotions combined with classroom management; keeping a relational perspective; supporting a temperament-based classroom management plan; focusing on culturally and developmentally appropriate classroom management strategies; and including participation-centered classroom management activities (Emmer & Sabornie, 2015; Martin et al., 2016).

Additional research revealed two responses that had not been identified previously to include reactive and proactive management (Aliakbari & Bozorgmanesh, 2015). When classroom management is reactive it greatly interferes with instruction because valuable time is spent on dealing with disruptive behaviors, which takes away from teaching and learning. Classroom management that is proactive ensures that structures are in place to create a positive learning environment by decreasing the chances for disruptive behaviors (Aliakbari & Bozorgmanesh, 2015).

Aliakbari and Bozorgmanesh (2015) recognize four outcomes of effective proactive classroom management. The first seeks to create order within the learning environment including the physical aspect. The second looks at proactive structures for dealing with misbehavior before problems are created. The third guarantees that appropriate instruction is planned and carried out, while the last outcome ensures that the emotional and cognitive needs of all students are addressed (Aliakbari & Bozorgmanesh, 2015).

Martin et al. (2016) believe that students must contribute to the creation and maintenance of positive learning environments that support academic learning as well as social and emotional learning. Four themes support the need for social emotional learning and the need to create positive learning environments to include the development of positive teacher and student relationships based on mutual respect, supporting the moral and social values of individuals, development of self-regulation skills, and creating a sense of connectedness within the learning community (Martin et al., 2016).

CREATING AN OPTIMAL CLASSROOM CLIMATE

Successful classroom management affects several components of a classroom that work together to create optimal teaching and learning opportunities. According to the Ministry of Education (2015), excellent classroom management provides support for efficient use of time and effective teaching. In the beginning of the school year, it is important for teachers to invest a sufficient amount of time to set the tone in their classroom (Responsive Classroom, 2018).

First, engage students in identifying meaningful and appropriate classroom rules and routines. When students take part in creating the rules and routines they have a vested interest in the learning environment, thus making the classroom a learning community (Responsive Classroom, 2018). This is first begun during morning meeting, and the rules and routines are implicitly and consistently taught and practiced throughout the first six weeks of school (Responsive Classroom, 2018). Doing this will help to build consistency and the rules, rituals, and routines ultimately become a natural part of the school day. As a result, teachers spend less time redirecting and correcting bad behaviors (Responsive Classroom, 2018).

When classroom management is under control, effective teaching can occur. A classroom that is disorganized and lacks consistency has a teacher that spends most of her time redirecting students, which interferes with instruction and lessens time on learning (Ministry of Education, 2015). Efficient classroom management strategies help to create organized learning environments conducive for teaching (Responsive Classroom, 2018).

Strong classroom management is a result of consistency, which is an important part of any classroom environment. Consistency provides students with the expectations they need to control behaviors, engage in appropriate interactions, and understand what is required of them (Ministry of Education,

2015). When consistency is in place, a classroom should be able to run the same regardless of whether the teacher is in the room. One way to ensure consistency is to align classroom expectations to school-wide behavior initiatives (Ministry of Education, 2015).

ASPECTS OF EFFECTIVE CLASSROOM MANAGEMENT

Martin et al. (2016) and Emmer and Sabornie (2015) both outline and support the five components of classroom management. The first, teacher emotions and classroom management, suggests that teachers must find ways to control their emotions while creating and maintaining an authoritative and caring image. Within this first factor some clarity is needed. Emotions constitute teacher actions and include body language, facial expressions, and verbal statements (Martin et al., 2016).

Teachers need to be completely aware of their self-presentation during interactions with students. Teacher behaviors, such as demeanors and personas, must embrace a supportive, yet authoritative ambiance, while teachers also must ensure that expectations are clearly stated to students so that there leaves no room for interpretation as to what is anticipated (Emmer & Sabornie, 2015; Martin et al., 2016).

Having a relational perspective, the second component, requires that teachers embrace an image of being both caring and authoritative (Emmer & Sabornie, 2015). Research has shown that students respond well to individuals who are compassionate and supportive but also maintain a level of authority (Martin et al., 2016). When creating an image of authority and care the emphasis needs to be on teacher actions rather than strategies or academics. Teachers need to consider taking on a social-emotional perspective supporting self-regulation, respect, and care. A teacher's actions, cognitions, and attitudes are key in supporting a relational perspective for classroom management (Emmer & Sabornie, 2015; Martin et al., 2016).

The third component, temperament-based classroom management, acknowledges the various student temperaments and responds by scaffolding appropriate proactive strategies (Emmer & Sabornie, 2015). When thinking about temperament in terms of students, it is important to note that this refers to a form of social processing. A student's temperament contributes to the way he or she views and interacts with his or her environment (Martin et al., 2016).

It is also important to understand that a teacher's temperament and behavior can influence the behaviors of certain students. Thus, teachers must tailor certain behaviors based upon the temperaments of various students (Emmer & Sabornie, 2015). This can be considered a form of differentiation. When the learning environment is responsive to a student's temperament he or she will blossom socially, emotionally, and academically (Martin et al., 2016).

Developmentally and culturally responsive classroom management is grounded in child development and cultural sensitivity theories, and focuses on providing appropriate and sensitive instructional approaches (Martin et al., 2016; Responsive Classroom, 2018).

It is well researched that a teacher's actions, or anyone's for that matter, are a result of their belief systems and experiences (Emmer & Sabornie, 2015; Martin et al., 2016). Beliefs, whether right or wrong, have a strong influence on a teacher's interactions with certain students. Two theoretical systems contribute to this frame of thought, those of behavior management and instructional management.

Behavior management, in this respect, refers to the planned efforts to prevent behaviors, including the teacher's response to any behaviors. Teachers must be proactive in this realm, involving the establishment of rules and routines, creating a reward and consequence structure, and involving input from students (Martin et al., 2016; Responsive Classroom, 2018). Instructional management consists of the methodologies and pedagogy implemented by the teacher. This involves proactively creating well-planned lessons, which include developmentally appropriate approaches, structured routines, monitoring transitions, and seatwork (Responsive Classroom, 2018; Martin et al., 2016).

Participation-centered classroom management compares the ideas of teacher-centered and student-centered approaches. First, the idea of teacher-centered methodologies focuses strictly on behavior management through an authoritative lens only. This type of method results in passive learning opportunities and offers the poorest results (Martin et al., 2016). Student-centered approaches, however, embrace a humanistic approach of active participation as learning occurs through engagement in social participation and interactions (Martin et al., 2016; Responsive Classroom, 2018).

Student-centered approaches create and support effective learning communities where both teachers and students are active participants. Through mutually created rituals and routines, individuals feel a sense of connectedness and belonging, as well as a piece of ownership in the community (Martin et al., 2016).

CLASSROOM MANAGEMENT AND STUDENT PERFORMANCE

Classroom management has several components that ensure a well-run and student-centered class where there are fewer distractions and learning opportunities for all students are the expectation not the exception (Aliakbari & Bozorgmanesh, 2015). Classroom management strategies should work to organize space, time, and materials, which will support both the social and academic behaviors of students (Aliakbari & Bozorgmanesh, 2015).

Classroom management strategies fall into two categories, proactive and reactive (Aliakbari & Bozorgmanesh, 2015). Using classroom management strategies to control student behaviors is often a reactive process, and teachers spend valuable time addressing disruptive behaviors and less time providing instruction. When strategies are used proactively, teachers are able to create supportive learning environments that address the academic and behavioral needs of all students (Aliakbari & Bozorgmanesh, 2015).

In their examination of the literature, Aliakbari and Bozorgmanesh (2015) identify several components of developing necessary classroom management. The authors use the expression classroom management as an umbrella term for managing the class, managing student behavior, and managing student learning.

Aliakbari and Bozorgmanesh (2015) stress that classroom management strategies should include establishing order, dealing with misbehavior, offering appropriate instruction, and addressing the emotional and cognitive needs of students. The organization of the classroom, managing teacher temperament and emotions, encouraging positive teacher-student relationships, and establishing punishment and reward systems are also critical to developing good classroom management (Aliakbari & Bozorgmanesh, 2015; Responsive Classroom, 2018).

SUPPORTING BOTH ACADEMIC AND SOCIAL-EMOTIONAL LEARNING THROUGH EFFECTIVE CLASSROOM MANAGEMENT

Research has proven a link between effective classroom management and positive academic and social-emotional learning of students (Martin et al., 2016). Positive classroom environments, created through proactive classroom management strategies, provide a powerful component to influence student behavior, student engagement, and the quality of student learning (Martin et al., 2016).

Further studies have revealed the positive impact of classroom management on teacher stress, burnout, job satisfaction, and retention efforts (Martin et al., 2016). This makes sense, as the less reactive a teacher has to be, the less time spent on redirecting student behavior, the more time a teacher has to engage in effective teaching (Responsive Classroom, 2018). When teachers are able to perform their job and make a difference in student outcomes, the chances are higher that they will remain in the field.

In their review of the literature, Martin et al. (2016) revealed four general themes to support effective classroom management for academic and social-emotional growth. These themes include developing positive teacher-student relationships consisting of mutual respect; supporting the moral and social values of all students as well as the school community; providing proactive approaches that support the development of self-regulation and connectedness within the learning environment; and offering effective classroom management strategies that can be altered based upon individual student characteristics, including developmental level and culture.

FINAL THOUGHTS

Successful classroom management combines setting rules and rituals, commonly referred to as classroom "norms," with input from students to proactively structure expectations so that effective teaching and learning can occur (Aliakbari & Bozorgmanesh, 2015; Emmer & Sabornie, 2015; Martin et al., 2016).

Critical to securing positive learning environments, the following components provide the basis for classroom expectations and include teacher emotions combined with classroom management: keeping a relational perspective; supporting a temperament-based classroom management plan; focusing on culturally and developmentally appropriate classroom management strategies; and including participation-centered classroom management activities (Emmer & Sabornie, 2015; Martin et al., 2016).

Aliakbari & Bozorgmanesh (2015) examined both reactive and proactive strategies and concluded that proactive strategies support better teaching and learning outcomes. There are four positive outcomes of proactive classroom management strategies, which include the creation of order within the learning environment, which provides structure, consistency, and security; the implementation of proactive structures for preventing disruptive behaviors; the occurrence of actively planning instruction that is developmentally and culturally appropriate; and the addressing of the emotional and cognitive needs of all students (Aliakbari & Bozorgmanesh, 2015).

Martin et al. (2016) studied classroom management as a way to support not only academic achievement but social emotional learning as well. This most successfully occurs when classrooms are created to be positive learning environments through well-structured classroom management techniques. Four themes emerged from their research, including the development of positive teacher-student relationships based on mutual respect, support for the moral and social values of individuals, the development of self-regulation skills, and ensuring a sense of connectedness within the learning community (Martin et al., 2016).

It is clear that proactive classroom management strategies support positive emotional, behavioral, and academic growth for all students (Responsive

Classroom, 2018). Input from students allows them to have a voice and take ownership in the learning community providing further evidence of the necessity for the development of positive relationships, developmentally and culturally appropriate structures, and consistency in implementation (Responsive Classroom, 2018).

POINTS TO REMEMBER

- Classroom management consists of proactively setting structures that establish order, addressing the emotional and cognitive needs of students, and supporting the development of positive relationships.
- Creating a positive learning environment supports the social emotional needs and academic growth of all students.
- For classroom management strategies to work, sufficient time must be spent in the beginning of the school year engaged in rehearsing the strategies. Practices and strategies must be implemented with fidelity and consistency across all school environments so that they become second nature.
- Effective classroom management strategies must be developmentally and culturally appropriate so that the learning environment will be accepting, and all students will have a sense of belonging and connectedness.

Chapter Five

Effective Instruction

Evidence-Based and High-Quality Practices

Today's classrooms are comprised of a diverse population of students from various cultural backgrounds and with different ability levels and learning styles, and, as a result, educators must use highly effective teaching strategies consistently (Hozien, 2017; Wells, Fox, & Cordova-Cobo, 2016). Evidence-based instructional practices have been proven highly effective by rigorous and extensive research studies (Maheady, Rafferty, Patti, & Budin, 2016; Scheeler, Budin, & Markelz, 2016). Furthermore, federal legislation mandates such as the Individuals with Disabilities Education Improvement Act (IDEA) and the Every Student Succeeds Act (ESSA), require the use of evidence-based instructional practices in an attempt to close the achievement gap (Samuels, 2016; American Psychological Association, 2017; ASCD, 2017).

Evidence-based instructional strategies help to close the achievement gap by ensuring that all students are exposed to and receive appropriate and highly effective instruction every day. The Council for Exceptional Children (2014) developed a set of five standards for categorizing evidence-based practices. Within each of the five standards, eight quality indicators must be met. What Works Clearinghouse (2015) has developed a similar set of categories and indicators for meeting the requirements of practices deserving the label of "evidence-based."

Commonly used evidence-based instructional practices found in schools today include direct teaching, setting high standards, differentiation, consistent use of formative assessment strategies, and implementation of Universal Design for Learning (CAST, 2018; Tomlinson, 2014; Stephens, 2015). These evidence-based practices can be utilized across all content areas and with all student populations (Archer & Hughes, 2011; Tomlinson, 2014).

Some instructional practices, although not identified as evidence based for one reason or another, may also be very beneficial for many students (Cook & Cook, 2013; Cook & Odom, 2013; Rosenshine, 2012). Non-evidence-based strategies that have shown positive student outcomes include the use of cognitive supports, breaking down information into manageable chunks, allowing sufficient time to master skills before moving onto the next task, extensive time to practice concepts, and the frequent use of questioning (Rosenshine, 2012).

THE EVIDENCE-BASED INSTRUCTIONAL PRACTICE MANDATE

According to the literature, the use of evidence-based, or research-based instructional practices, can help to close the achievement gap (Graham, Harris, & Chambers, 2016; Meadows Center for Preventing Educational Risk & George W. Bush Institute, 2016). Research-based strategies provide high-quality instruction focused on specific skill development for students in need and across curricular content areas (What Works Clearinghouse, 2017). Federally mandated use of evidence-based instructional strategies, along with specific agencies and professional development opportunities, provide resources and assistance for educators to ensure the consistent and appropriate use of these practices (Samuels, 2016; What Works Clearinghouse, 2017).

Federal mandates also require that teachers be highly qualified in the specific content areas in which they teach and licensed by the state in which they work (Samuels, 2016). To obtain a teaching license, there are various qualifications a teacher candidate must meet, such as passing teacher exams, meeting core competencies, completing an educator preparation program, engaging in a student-teaching or practicum experience, and obtaining a master's degree in education (Samuels, 2016). Incorporated within each of these components are exposure to evidence-based instructional practices.

WHAT MAKES AN INSTRUCTIONAL PRACTICE EVIDENCE BASED?

According to the U.S. Department of Education Institute of Educational Sciences (2003) and the Council for Exceptional Children (2014), there are two criteria that must be met in order for an instructional practice to be considered evidence based; the first requires extensive and rigorous research studies showing positive student outcomes, while the second requires that the conclusions must indicate promising results for a specific population of students and/or a skill area (Cook et al., 2015; Council for Exceptional Children, 2014).

The Council for Exceptional Children (2014) along with What Works Clearinghouse (2015) have developed standards for indicating which instructional practices can be considered evidence based. Within the Council for Exceptional Children (2014) standards, there are eight quality indicators, which include context and setting, participants, intervention agents, description of the practice, implementation fidelity, internal validity, outcome measures and dependent variables, and data analysis (Council for Exceptional Children, 2014).

The classifications include five identities to include evidence-based practices, potentially evidence-based practices, practices having mixed effects, practices having negative effects, and practices having insufficient evidence to categorize effectiveness (Browder, Wood, Thompson, & Ribuffo, 2014; Council for Exceptional Children, 2014). All eight indicators must be met in order for an instructional practice to be considered evidence based (Council for Exceptional Children, 2014; Cook, et al., 2015; Harn, Parisi, & Stoolmiller, 2013).

- Context and setting: provides a thorough description of critical features, such as study demographics, participant demographics, and the intervention and/or curriculum.
- Intervention agent: ensures that the study documents the researchers, including their qualifications and training, and any background variables with regard to the researchers.
- Description of practice: documents the methodical evidence of the study, including the researcher's role and responsibility.
- Implementation fidelity: confirms that the study was conducted with fidelity, through reliable measures and thorough documentation.
- Internal validity: guarantees that the study is well documented including the conditions and interventions implemented, and ensures that the independent variable was under the control of the researcher. Further, this indicator must clearly describe if there are comparison groups or if it is single-subject.
- Outcome measures and dependent variables: assures that the study outcomes are directly linked to positive academic achievement.
- Data analysis: confirms that appropriate data analysis steps have been implemented and reports accurate results and effect sizes. (Council for Exceptional Children, 2014; Cook et al., 2015; Browder et al., 2014).

These quality indicators are used to categorize instructional practices into the five evidence-based practice standards mentioned earlier. Further investigation of each of the five practice standards indicates clearly defined groupings to classify strategies and practices.

- Evidence-based practice standard: includes practices that have indicated positive effects from two or more methodologically sound comparison studies.
- Potentially evidence-based practice standard: reflects interventions that are supported by one to three methodologically sound comparison studies or as an alternative two to four single-subject studies.
- Mixed-evidence practice standard: requires a ratio of at least 2:1 of methodologically sound studies indicating positive to neutral effects.
- Insufficient practice standard: does not produce sufficient results to meet any of the practice standards.
- Negative-results practice standard: includes practices that indicate negative effects, or the negative effects overshadow any positive effects. (Browder et al., 2014; Council for Exceptional Children, 2014; Cook et al., 2015).

COMMONLY IMPLEMENTED EVIDENCE-BASED PRACTICES

Research has identified many effective evidence-based practices that support increased performance in specific academic areas as well as others that can be implemented across all content areas (Archer & Hughes, 2011; Stephens, 2015). Commonly implemented evidence-based practices that can be applied within any content area to increase student achievement include direct teaching, gradual release, setting high expectations, differentiated instruction, and Universal Design for Learning (UDL) (CAST, 2018; Archer & Hughes, 2011; Stephens, 2015).

Direct teaching. Direct teaching, also referred to as explicit teaching, is a well-studied strategy (Archer & Hughes, 2011). When using direct instruction, the teacher clearly models the learning process while providing supports for students (Archer & Hughes, 2011). One direct teaching model is known as gradual release, also referred to as *I do, We do, You Do*. This model is based loosely on Vygotsky's Zone of Proximal Development theory, which suggests that students should be faced with tasks that they can achieve with support and build from there (Archer & Hughes, 2011).

Within the gradual-release model, there are four stages: focused lessons, guided instruction, collaborative instruction, and independent learning (Archer & Hughes, 2011). Focused lessons involve connecting concepts to previously learned concepts and the teacher explicitly modeling the new skill or concept and providing sufficient instructional time before moving on to the second stage (Archer & Hughes, 2011). Guided instruction provides students with ongoing support from the teacher, including encouragement, practice, and effort (Archer & Hughes, 2011).

Collaborative learning engages students in group or pair activities. During this stage, students are practicing and rehearsing the new skill with peer-to-peer modeling and discourse (Archer & Hughes, 2011). It is extremely important that students comprehend the skill or concept before moving into the fourth stage of independent practice (Archer & Hughes, 2011). Within this final stage, students are actively applying new concepts to various situations and, in addition, students are able to transfer their learning to other areas (Archer & Hughes, 2011).

Setting high expectations. Setting high expectations has proven to build student confidence and independence when implemented in any learning environment (Stephens, 2015). High expectations can promote academic and social growth and often offers students a chance to have a voice in deciding what behaviors, rules, and rituals should be set (Stephens, 2015).

When setting expectations, specific behaviors need to be clearly identified and stated to all individuals within the learning community and across all settings. All stakeholders including students, teachers, administrators, and staff, must be aware of and practice the expectations in order to ensure consistency and support (Stephens, 2015).

Differentiated instruction. Differentiated instruction is a strategy that takes into account the needs, abilities, interests, and learning styles of all students and aims to highlight strengths and accommodate for weaknesses (Scruggs, Mastropieri, & Marshak, 2012; Tomlinson, 2014). Through differentiation, instructional techniques, assessment strategies, and assignments are offered in various forms to match the diverse needs within the classroom (Obiakor, Harris, Mutua, Rotatori, & Algozzine, 2012).

Universal design for learning (UDL). UDL is a proactive approach to providing differentiated instruction. Based upon research in the fields of neuroscience and education, UDL offers students choices and supports that are based upon the way the human brain learns (Meyer, Rose, & Gordon, 2014; CAST, 2018).

UDL is based on three principles that include multiple means of representation, multiple means of expression, and multiple means of engagement (National Center of Universal Design for Learning, 2017). Multiple means of representation accounts for several ways to present new information to students (CAST, 2018). Some examples include using visuals, videos, and auditory presentations.

Providing students variety in the way they can demonstrate comprehension of the lesson supports executive function and is the heart of multiple means of expression (CAST, 2018). Teachers who offer more than one way to assess learning, by finding the best bet for student learning style and strength, exemplify this principle (Meyer, Rose, & Gordon, 2014; National Center of Universal Design for Learning, 2017).

The multiple means of engagement principle works to ensure students are interested in the learning process, motivated to engage in academic work, and display effort to achieve goals (CAST, 2018). Teachers can support this element by connecting concepts to each student's background and/or interests while offering flexible grouping or activities to further engagement and make the learning experience more enjoyable (Meyer, Rose, & Gordon, 2014; National Center of Universal Design for Learning, 2017).

Formative assessment. Formative assessment is the collection, analysis, and interpretation of student data (Nicol & Macfarlane, 2006). Teachers use the data from formative assessment to drive future instruction for all students. Formative assessment seeks to determine student comprehension, identify misconceptions, identify concepts that need to be re-taught, and track student progress (Nicol & Macfarlane, 2006).

Nicol & Macfarlane (2006) identified five criteria for effective formative assessment practices. The first requires that formative assessment be aligned to the learning objectives. The second accounts for the frequency and authenticity of the assessment strategies used. The third criteria is ensuring the consistency of corrective feedback and support based upon the results of the formative assessment data. The fourth criteria takes into account that both self and peer assessment is part of the formative process, while the final criteria supports the belief that multiple forms of assessment should be offered. This provides students with choices to demonstrate their learning (Nicol & Macfarlane, 2006).

HIGH-QUALITY AND EFFECTIVE INSTRUCTIONAL STRATEGIES

Up until this point, we have discussed the benefits of evidence-based instructional practices; however, not all instructional strategies are identified as evidence based, yet many that are not are able to produce positive results for a vast majority of students (Cook & Cook, 2013; Sornson, 2015). These strategies are commonly referred to as high-quality instructional practices (Cook & Odom, 2013; Sornson, 2015)

Research conducted by Rosenshine (2012) focused on the cognitive sciences and how best to support students when learning new content. Specifically, Rosenshine (2012), examined how to support the working memory while transferring information into longer-term memory storage. The limitations of working memory make it necessary to provide cognitive supports to assist students within the learning process (Rosenshine, 2012). These findings were then taken into consideration while researching master teachers and the strategies that were implemented consistently to improve student performance (Rosenshine, 2012).

Rosenshine (2012) took the evidence gathered and identified components of instruction that focused on providing cognitive supports that were essential for advancing student learning. The components included connecting concepts, presenting information in small chunks, asking the right questions, providing exemplars and sufficient teacher modeling, sufficient time to practice, frequent check-ins, scaffolding, and independent practice.

Connecting concepts. The idea of connecting concepts sets the stage for better long-term memory storage (Rosenshine, 2012). Before introducing new information, teachers should spend time reviewing previously learned concepts, as this will help with greater transfer and retrieval later on. Similarly, presenting concepts in smaller chunks avoids working memory overload, which can slow down the processing speed and result in frustration (Rosenshine, 2012). By breaking concepts into smaller chunks, students can spend sufficient time engaged in practicing those skills prior to moving on to the next.

Questioning. Asking students the right questions helps to support cognitive growth, especially when the questions engage students in explaining their thought process (Rosenshine, 2012). Providing students with exemplars and sufficient teacher modeling provides the necessary cognitive supports to help students master new skills. One extremely beneficial way teachers can model for students is through the use of think-alouds as they provide students with insight into the cognitive process involved in mastering a skill (Ness, 2018). In a think-aloud, the teacher models the thinking that goes into solving a problem or answering a question so that the next time, the student is able to complete the task independently (Ness, 2018).

Increased time for independent and supported practice. Providing students with increased time to engage in independent and supported practice increases the transfer of information from working memory to long-term memory (Rosenshine, 2012). When students engage in additional time to process, rehearse, and use new information, the mastery of new skills is cemented. When students have a concrete understanding of foundational skills, it allows for rapid recall and greater cognitive energy to be devoted to other tasks such as comprehension of new skills (Rosenshine, 2012).Teachers can support this in activities that ask students to summarize and elaborate on newly learned skills.

Frequent check-ins. Research has proven that when teachers frequently check-in with their students throughout the learning process it plays a significant role in moving information from working memory to long-term memory storage (Rosenshine, 2012). Through questioning techniques or other formative assessment strategies, misconceptions can be identified and appropriate re-teaching is possible.

Scaffolding. Providing scaffolds for students allows temporary supports to assist with comprehension of new material or skills. Rosenshine (2012) refers to scaffolds as cognitive apprenticeships. Some examples include providing students with checklists, graphic organizers, completed work examples, and teacher modeling (Alber, 2016). Once students have gained enough confidence to attend to tasks independently, the scaffolds can be slowly taken away.

FINAL THOUGHTS

With the diversity in today's classrooms, the ability of teachers to implement highly effective instructional strategies is critical to the success of our students. Evidence-based instructional practices, mandated by federal regulations, have been proven highly effective through extensive research and indicate consistent positive results (Samuels, 2016). Evidence-based teaching strategies have been proven as highly effective at closing the achievement gap by providing all students with appropriate, and individualized, instruction (Maheady et al., 2016; Scheeler et al., 2016).

Evidence-based practice standards have been developed by both the Council for Exceptional Children (2014) and What Works Clearinghouse (2015). The professional standards assist researchers with identification and classification of instructional practice along the continuum of being labeled as evidence based (Browder et al., 2014; Cook et al., 2015).

Even though many instructional strategies may not be labeled as evidence based, they are still considered highly effective at promoting and supporting student achievement (Cook & Cook, 2013; Cook & Odom, 2013; Rosenshine, 2012; Sornson, 2015). Examples of high-quality instructional practices include the use of cognitive supports, breaking down information into manageable chunks, allowing sufficient time to master skills before moving onto the next task, extensive time to practice concepts, and the frequent use of questioning (Rosenshine, 2012).

POINTS TO REMEMBER

- Evidence-based instructional practices are mandated by federal regulations, including the Individuals with Disabilities Education Improvement Act (2004) and the Every Student Succeeds Act (2015). Federal agencies provide resources to educators to ensure that this mandate is carried out.
- The Council for Exceptional Children (2014) along with What Works Clearinghouse (2015) have developed, separately, professional standards for identifying and classifying instructional practices as evidence-based.

Instructional practices must meet specific quality indicators to place them within the highest level of the standards and label them as evidence based.
- Much research has been conducted on the effectiveness of implementing evidence-based instructional strategies. These practices are highly effective at closing the achievement gap by providing all students with appropriate instruction.
- Some teaching practices, supported by extensive research, may not be labeled as evidence based but contribute to the increase in student achievement. These practices are known as high-quality teaching practices and should be implemented consistently within all learning environments.

Chapter Six

Promoting Student Engagement

Setting the Conditions for Success

Student engagement is key to addressing low achievement, student boredom, and high dropout rates (Martin & Torres, 2015). The literature shows that student engagement declines during the progression from the elementary grades into middle school and through high school (Martin & Torres, 2015). It is estimated that 40 to 60% of high school students are disengaged in the learning process (Martin & Torres, 2015). Student engagement combines an emotional, behavioral, and cognitive commitment to build interest and meaningful involvement in the learning process (Marzano Center, 2015).

It is believed that the relationships and connections that students have within the school environment support the increase in student engagement and motivation (Martin & Torres, 2015; Marzano Center, 2015). According to Stephens (2015), motivation and engagement go hand in hand to increase academic achievement and involve the work of the teacher as well as the student. Through the building of positive relationships, support of intrinsic desires, and embracing an affective demeanor, student engagement can be increased (Marzano Center, 2015).

When it comes to engaging and motivating diverse learners, the most effective strategy is providing choices, as it increases student effort, taps into intrinsic motivation, increases task performance, and elevates student learning (Marzano & Pickering, 2010). There are five strategies that are highly effective at increasing student engagement: high-energy classrooms, missing information, mild competition, supporting self-esteem, and providing small amounts of pressure (Marzano Center, 2015).

Marzano & Pickering (2010) explored the idea of emotional engagement, suggesting that this is supported through relational aspects within the school and classroom community. Emotional engagement is created, nurtured, and maintained through positive relationships between teacher and student, teacher to teacher, and student to student (Marzano & Pickering, 2010).

Additional research identified seven ways that teachers can support positive student engagement and motivation within their classrooms (Stephens, 2015). The first ensures that teachers take care of their own health and mental well-being. Next, educators should create a welcoming and accepting classroom environment. The third component suggests that teachers who support students' self-beliefs increase their confidence and self-esteem, while the fourth practice involves getting to know their students. This can be accomplished through surveys, questionnaires, and or individual conferences. Student autonomy is another critical component of creating a positive learning environment. The final two aspects include active collaboration during learning opportunities and offering students challenging activities (Stephens, 2015).

DEFINING STUDENT ENGAGEMENT

According to the Marzano Center (2015), student engagement combines both interest and meaningful involvement. When students are interested in the topic in which they are learning, they are naturally more involved and focus more attention on absorbing the content (Martin & Torres, 2015). Student engagement is multidimensional, combining emotional, behavioral, and cognitive engagement and provides both positive and negative reactions to others (Martin & Torres, 2015). Behavioral engagement supports participation in academic, social, and co-curricular activities, while cognitive engagement is the student's level of investment in the learning process (Martin & Torres, 2015).

Student engagement embraces multidimensional relationships; thus, students have various connections throughout the school environment such as the school community, teachers, their peers, the curriculum, and instructional strategies (Martin & Torres, 2015; Marzano Center, 2015). These relationships combine to meet the emotional, behavioral, and cognitive needs of all students and when these relationships are positive, nurturing, and supportive, the whole student thrives (Martin & Torres, 2015).

The Marzano Center (2015) developed five strategies for increasing student engagement: high-energy classrooms, missing information, competition, self-system, and mild pressure. Research confirms that the same part of the brain that focuses on learning also focuses on movement; thus, high energy classrooms engage in frequent movement (Marzano Center 2015). Movement can be incorporated in many ways, from simply using a highlighter to mark certain information on a page to whole body movements, such as playing four corners to cast a vote in a classroom debate scenario.

The next strategy, missing information, suggests incorporating puzzles and games into learning as a way to entice students with anticipation (Marzano Center, 2015). Any academic games, such as scavenger hunts and word finds, would work to meet the goal of this strategy. The third strategy, competition, provides opportunities to add excitement and fun into the learning process (Marzano Center, 2015). Competition in the form of team problem-solving, games such as Jeopardy, and debates, allow students to engage in friendly and structured matches. It is important to note that teachers should ensure that all students have a chance to be on a winning team; therefore, careful selection of groups or teams is critical (Marzano Center, 2015).

The fourth tactic, self-system, requires that teachers consider the interests and backgrounds of their students so that value in learning is perceived (Marzano Center, 2015). When teachers proactively plan by taking the time to learn about their students, through questionnaires and interest inventories, they provide students with enjoyment, satisfaction, and pride during the learning process (Marzano Center, 2015). The final strategy, mild pressure, keeps students' attention by keeping them guessing and on their toes. Teachers can use effective questioning techniques, cold-calling, and frequent student check-ins to accomplish the practice of mild pressure (Marzano Center, 2015).

MOTIVATION AND ENGAGEMENT

According to Stephens (2015), motivation and engagement are comprised of a student's energy, drive to learn, and achievement. Motivation and engagement both play a role in student achievement; however, it can also present challenges for teachers. The more engaged students are, the higher their academic performance and the fewer the incidents of disruptive behaviors (Stephens, 2015).

Similar to Martin and Torres (2016), Stephens (2015) agreed that student engagement combines behavioral, emotional, and cognitive commitment within the learning process. When students are engaged, they demonstrate more effort, display positive emotions, have more attention, display higher grades, and have lower dropout rates (Stephens, 2015).

Student engagement and motivation is both an intrinsic and extrinsic process that requires the work and dedication of the teacher as well as the student (Stephens, 2015). Teachers can support and increase this intrinsic inspiration through their pedagogy, displaying confidence as an educator, and having an affective orientation (Stephens, 2015).

Teachers who support student autonomy facilitate greater motivation, curiosity, and desire (Stephens, 2015). Creating and nurturing positive teacher-student relationships helps to support emotional, behavioral, and cognitive engagement, as well as increase language development. When it comes to an affective orientation, students who perceive the teacher as being a caring individual tend to learn more (Stephens, 2015).

PROVIDING CHOICES

Incorporating choices within a classroom learning environment begins with engaging students in developing rules, rituals, and routines (Marzano & Pickering, 2010). Responsive classrooms do this as part of their regular daily routine. Classrooms that engage in including students in articulating both desired and undesired behaviors allow students to use their voices in a positive way within the classroom community (Responsive Classroom, 2018; Marzano & Pickering, 2010).

Teachers can provide students with many choices and in various forms such as task choices and alternatives in report formatting. When choices are given to students, they are able to take control of their learning and design their own educational goals (Marzano & Pickering, 2010). When students have the academic freedom to choose their independent tasks, teachers have provided options that appeal to a variety of different learning styles and ability levels.

Reporting format options might include written, verbal, and digital outputs (Marzano & Pickering, 2010). Teachers who choose to use an array of reporting options can ensure specific standards are met by providing all students with the same performance criteria and expectations. These can be presented and supported through the use of rubrics and exemplars.

EMOTIONAL ENGAGEMENT

Emotional engagement considers the relational aspects within the learning community. Teacher to teacher, teacher to student, and student to student are three different types of relationships found within an educational setting. Specifically focusing on the teacher-to-student relationship, positive interactions can greatly increase student engagement and achievement (Marzano & Pickering, 2010).

Teachers who display positive demeanors and engage in enthusiastic teaching styles have a better chance of promoting, nurturing, and sustaining encouraging teacher-to-student relationships (Marzano & Pickering, 2010). Teachers who encourage strong relationships also consider instructional decisions as ways to support and cherish these connections.

In relation to instructional decisions that support positive relationships, teachers must make decisions based on four symbolic questions (Marzano & Pickering, 2010). The first two questions, "How do I feel?" and "Am I interested?" focus the attention on the student, while the other two questions, "Is this important?" and "Can I do this?" gauge a student's interest in the topic (Marzano & Pickering, 2010). Teachers must consider these questions when planning their instruction and student choices in order to secure relationships and heighten student engagement and interest, which will support increased student performance (Marzano & Pickering, 2010).

PACING

Pacing refers to the flow of a lesson, which greatly influences the engagement and interest of students (Marzano & Pickering, 2010). When a lesson's pacing is too slow, students' energy levels and attention drop; however, when the pacing of a lesson is too fast, students tend to get frustrated and confused—both cause interferences with engagement (Marzano & Pickering, 2010). In order to ensure balanced pacing occurs, teachers need to proactively plan, including how to present new content, individual and group work strategies, and transitions (Marzano & Pickering, 2010).

WHOLE-GROUP STUDENT ENGAGEMENT STRATEGIES

When classrooms are engaged in whole-group instruction, it is important to have strategies to ensure that increased participation, student engagement, active learning, and self-evaluation occur, while preventing behavior problems (Nagro, Hooks, Fraser, & Cornelius, 2016). To maintain active participation and engagement in the lesson, teachers should provide high rates of opportunity and prompting of all students to respond (Nagro et al., 2016).

To encourage active participation, teachers should consider using whole-group response systems, such as white boards, hand signals, and student response systems (Byrne, 2014). Another way to engage students is through peer interactions, such as *turn and talk* or *think, pair, share* (Lemov, 2015) It is important for teachers to closely monitor the engagement of lower-achieving students compared to higher-achieving students. One way to ensure equal engagement would be to pair students of varying abilities (Nagro et al., 2016).

WHAT TEACHERS CAN DO TO ENSURE THEIR CLASSROOMS SUPPORT POSITIVE STUDENT ENGAGEMENT

Stephens (2015) identified seven ways that teachers can help support student engagement. As a first line of defense, teachers must take care of their mental and physical health as well as have safe outlets for stress relief (Stephens, 2015). Beyond self-care, teachers should ensure that their classrooms are welcoming and accepting of all students, including those with disabilities and those from various cultural backgrounds (Young, Michael, & Citro, 2018). Classroom environments that are warm, inviting, and accommodating support the cognitive, social, and emotional needs of all students.

Supporting students' self-beliefs is a positive way to increase engagement (Stephens, 2015). Engagement increases when students feel that they are in charge of their learning, and as a result, students begin to believe that they can reach their learning goals, as well as deal with failure. Teachers can encourage this by engaging in activities that promote problem solving (Stephens, 2015).

In the beginning of the school year, surveying students through questionnaires or interviews, about their likes and dislikes, provides information that teachers can use to connect content to student interests (Stephens, 2015; Balasubramanian, Jaykumar, & Fukey, 2014). Teachers need to evaluate the curriculum and content in conjunction with student interests in order to make it meaningful to students and to increase motivation.

Student autonomy is another way to increase engagement and motivation. Allowing students to work autonomously through learning relationships with their peers, allows them to gain competence in reaching their educational goals (Hocket & Doubet, 2017). As an added bonus, independence fosters self-determination and supports intrinsic motivation (Stephens, 2015). Creating learning opportunities that encompass active collaboration promotes positive learning relationships, socialization, and development of peer relationships. Through active learning opportunities, student engagement and motivation are encouraged, supported, and maintained (Stephens, 2015).

Offering challenging learning activities that enrich and extend academic abilities is critical for increasing engagement and motivation (Stephens, 2015). When students are challenged to think critically, make connections, and evaluate new information, they are fully engaged in the learning process (Watanabe-Crockett, 2017). Teachers can support a variety of abilities by pairing up students to support one another through the learning process (Stephens, 2015).

FINAL THOUGHTS

According to Stephens (2015), motivation and engagement go hand in hand to increase academic achievement. As students progress through the grades, their level of engagement decreases, which directly affects motivation and academic achievement and contributes to the dropout rate (Martin & Torres, 2016). Student engagement is a combination of emotional, behavioral, and cognitive investments used to increase interest and meaningful involvement in the learning process (Marzano Center, 2015).

For schools, and particularly teachers, to sustain student engagement and motivation, the need for positive relationships within the school environment is critical (Martin & Torres, 2016; Marzano Center, 2015). To increase and maintain student engagement, teachers and students must work together to create and nurture mutually respectful relationships. Teachers should support the intrinsic desires of their students, while embracing an affective demeanor (Marzano Center, 2015).

Providing choices for students is quite possibly the best way to increase and support engagement and motivation for students during the learning process and beyond (Marzano & Pickering, 2010). Marzano & Pickering (2010) have identified, through much research, five strategies that are highly effective at increasing student engagement.

Research conducted by Stephens (2015) identified several ways teachers can increase positive student engagement and increase motivation within schools. Teachers who take care of their own health and mental well-being are better able to positively deal with the stress of being a teacher and present as stable and influential. Creating open and welcoming classroom environments ensures that students feel safe, secure, and accepted to take those educational and social risks. Encouraging students to believe in their abilities will ultimately increase their confidence and build self-esteem (Stephens, 2015).

When teachers get to know their students, it creates a sense of investment. Students believe that the teacher really cares about their well-being and will support their overall development. Encouraging student autonomy is another critical component of creating a positive learning environment (Hocket & Doubet, 2017). When students are empowered to take learning into their own hands, it increases individual responsibility and increases engagement. Supporting active learning through collaborative activities and presenting students with challenging activities increases motivation and engagement and sets the stage for success (Stephens, 2015).

POINTS TO REMEMBER

- It is estimated that 40 to 60% of high school students are disengaged from the learning process. Research indicates that as students progress through the grades, their levels of engagement and motivation drastically decrease.
- Student engagement is considered to be multidimensional, combining emotional, behavioral, and cognitive commitments. Three components work together to motivate students, pique their interests, and support academic performance and social growth.
- The most effective way to increase engagement and motivation in learning is to provide students with choices for task engagement and reporting formats or assessment strategies, among other things. Providing students with choices supports academic freedom and various learning styles.
- Emotional engagement plays a key role in the development of motivation and performance and is supported and nurtured by the positive relationships students develop within the school community.

Chapter Seven

Using Assessment Wisely

Creating, Analyzing, and Moving Forward from Data

Student assessment provides interpretative information to teachers and leaders about their impact on students and provides a lens through which to view myriad instructional methods (Hattie, 2015). Although assessment is often used to inform students of their progress, it is critical to use gathered data to apprise teachers of their impact on students (Alber, 2017; Hattie, 2015).

Assessments can be powerful tools when they are timely, informative, and related to what teachers are actually teaching in the classroom (Hattie, 2015; Conley, 2014). Schools are flooded with data, and adding more tests and assessments adds little more than a distraction. As it is, the results of the tests and their impact on students are all that really matters to teachers. Most agree that what is really needed is better interpretation of the collected data (Hattie, 2015; National Association of Elementary School Principals, 2011).

Educators need to understand what each student already knows, what they still need to know, and where that student needs to go next in the teaching process (National Association of Elementary School Principals, 2011). Successful teachers need to assess the visible impact they have on students, monitor learning, seek feedback about their teaching, and then evaluate and adjust their teaching methods based on these findings (Alber, 2017; Hattie, 2015).

Teachers can use data to identify individual student needs and place students in groups, interventions, and classrooms as well as monitor overall student progress, customize learning opportunities for individual students, and move students into or out of programs such as special education programs (Alber, 2017; Dougherty, 2015). Data results will help teachers modify curriculum and instruction, identify learning objectives that students have not learned and must be re-taught, and recognize individual and group success (National Association of Elementary School Principals, 2011; Dougherty, 2015).

Data can also be used to help school administrators coach and supervise teachers, guide discussions, and inform teachers of their strengths and weaknesses. New programs can be piloted, and assessment data can assist in communicating with parents when their students need additional academic or behavioral assistance. Looking back at past data can assist in evaluating expected outcomes (Dougherty, 2015).

SOURCES OF STUDENT DATA

Schools gather several types of data that are used in myriad ways. Formative assessments, such as standardized testing, unearths district, school, and grade-level data, while individual summative assessments provide teachers information on student performance in their individual classes (Fuglei, 2014). Summative and formative assessments, used in conjunction, can provide teachers feedback on classroom instruction and allow them to collect data from various sources including their own observations, cumulative files, and standardized test scores (Fuglei, 2014; Alber, 2017).

By using a variety of assessment methods during any given school week, teachers can obtain a more succinct view of what students know and understand. Using at least one formative assessment daily enables teachers to evaluate and assess the quality of learning taking place in the classroom and gain knowledge on how the student is evolving as a learner and what they, the teachers, need to do to assist the student in becoming successful (Dodge, 2017; National Association of Elementary School Principals, 2011).

Formative Assessments

Formative assessments support learning during the learning process by checking for student understanding and providing student feedback all while guiding teacher decision-making about future instruction (National Association of Elementary School Principals, 2011). Students should strive to understand what success looks like and use each assessment to understand how to improve (Dodge, 2017).

One of the most useful and informative ways to collect student data is through the use of formative assessments. These assessments include standardized testing, exit slips, brief quizzes and what is commonly known as thumbs up/thumbs down (Dwyer & William, 2017; Alber, 2017). Formative assessments are used to elicit, interpret, and make decisions about the next steps in instruction that may be more effective than previous decisions (Dwyer & William, 2017).

Data from standardized testing gives administrators and teachers a global view of their students by gauging overall learning and identifying knowledge gaps (Fuglei, 2014; National Association of Elementary School Principals, 2011). While administrators use formative data to address curricular or teaching insufficiency, teachers use knowledge gap information to identify subjects that need additional teaching time and to create individual assessments (Dwyer & William, 2017; Fuglei, 2014). Analytical assessment software can also help teachers anticipate student skill gaps and arrange classes to enhance individualized student learning (Fuglei, 2014).

Teachers also use standardized test results along with other data, such as in-class assignments and observations, to assist them in making instructional decisions (National Association of Elementary School Principals, 2011). Test results may be shared directly with individual students to set obtainable and realistic goals that can be met before the next test. Equally important, test data can reveal at what level students performed, inform decisions on student groupings, and the creation of seating charts (Alber, 2017).

Once teachers have data from standardized assessments, they can move forward and conduct individual assessments on new students to confirm those standardized findings and acknowledge individual student needs (Fuglei, 2014). These new data provide teachers with a comprehensive understanding of their students' personalities and abilities as well as insight into their learning styles (Fuglei, 2014). Teachers are then able to broaden curriculum goals and modify instruction to reflect individual student needs (Fuglei, 2014).

Summative Assessments

Summative assessments, such as grades on final assignments or projects, essays, and exams, are the most frequently used measure of student learning by teachers (Fuglei, 2014). This type of data provides information about individual student function and classroom performance, in other words, what a student can do right now or what they have learned throughout a particular unit of study. It can be particularly useful in assisting teachers to identify learning roadblocks or overall curriculum dysfunction (Dwyer & William, 2017; Fuglei, 2014).

When an entire class performs poorly, teachers can use information gathered from the data to reexamine their teaching process to see if the student gap is a result of failing to connect students with the material. Teachers are thus motivated to revise or restructure class materials or teaching strategies to ensure student learning goals and outcomes are met (Fuglei, 2014).

Summative assessments allow teachers to measure the growth of individual and whole-group learning, or in other words, how much learning has taken place (Alber, 2017; Dodge, 2017). If a large number of students do not do well on an exam, for example, teachers can reflect back on their lessons and teaching to reteach a lesson and/or make any necessary adjustments for the future (Alber, 2017). A teacher's own observations can help him or her learn how well students are making sense of the content and who may be struggling (Alber, 2017).

Reading student cumulative files can provide invaluable knowledge to teachers who may learn that the student who often missed class was actually homeless, while the student who acted bored was actually a gifted student that was inaccurately placed in a general education class (Alber, 2017). Having this type of knowledge will give teachers the opportunity to be empathetic, acknowledge the student's hardship, and collaboratively set goals for academic improvement as well as refer students for counseling services or advocate for additional support as needed (Alber, 2017).

Macrodata and Microdata

Although teachers use data to improve teaching, the data they collect also provide students with information that helps them become better learners and take greater ownership of their learning (Venables, 2017; Dyer, 2014). Macrodata, such as tables and bar graphs, reflect student performance on high-stakes assessments and are utilized in analyzing achievement trends across classes and grade levels to broadly demonstrate student achievement (Venables, 2017; Dyer, 2014). Microdata help obtain a clear sense of what is happening as students learn and identify gaps in learning (Venables, 2017).

There are also many sources of daily classroom microdata that are invaluable to informing instruction and help teachers make modifications to their instructional methods (Venables, 2017). These sources not only help teachers make modifications to their instruction methods but allow teachers to be proactive in their instruction rather than reactive, as done when responding to macrodata (Venables, 2017).

Warm-up questions. Bell ringers, or warm-up activities, provide teachers with information about the extent to which students understood the previously learned material. When used to start a lesson, students have the opportunity to show what they have learned about a topic with a particular focus. Activating students' background knowledge is one way to pay credence to what they know, help them recognize what they might still need to know, and answer any unanswered questions.

Warm-up questions can also be a quick review of challenging material or a check-in on what happened the previous week (Dyer, 2014). Depending on how well the students do, teachers can respond to student success or lack of understanding to adjust their instruction for the day (Venables, 2017).

Checks for understanding. During daily lessons, teachers receive data on where their students are in their learning from student responses to questions. Using No-Hands-Up techniques or All-Student Response systems allows students the opportunity to check their own understanding of a topic, compare their response with those of their peers, and hear the reasoning behind other responses so they can make adjustments to their own thinking (Lemov, 2015).

In some cases, the use of response questions may lead to skewed data that does not represent the class's mastery as a whole, as three or four students may be the only ones answering all the questions. To lessen this likelihood, teachers may have students respond to global questions using individual whiteboards or virtual student response systems in order to quickly assess the progress of all students during instruction (Venables, 2017; Byrne, 2014). Some teachers have also found it successful and effective to use electronic devices, such as clickers, iPads, and cell phones to measure student understanding (Byrne, 2014; Venables, 2017).

Homework. Meaningful homework assignments can also provide teachers with valuable data as well as work undertaken right in the classroom. Homework can help students determine what they know and what they don't know and position them to ask follow-up questions to help them figure out what they will do about it (Dyer, 2014). Providing students the opportunity to practice in class provides a learning environment where they can obtain instant help from the teacher or peer mentors (Dyer, 2014).

Homework and in-class work allows students to practice and tackle ideas learned during class instruction while demonstrating self-regulation (Venables, 2017; Dyer, 2014). When teachers circulate around the room while students are completing in-class work, they are not only able to assess student understanding and suggest additional learning tactics, but to immediately determine how effective their lesson and teaching methods were (Lemov, 2015; Venables, 2017).

Teachers may want to ask students to write content-specific summaries and reflections of material so that they have time to stop, reflect, make sense of the material they are being asked to learn, and/or derive personal meaning from their learning experiences (Dodge, 2017). Lists, charts, and graphic organizers are useful in that they provide students with an opportunity to organize information, make connections, and note any relationships between information (Dodge, 2017; Alber, 2016).

Students should be encouraged to use both words and pictures to make connections and increase memory, as it will help facilitate the retrieval of information in the future (Dodge, 2017). Using both words and pictures will also assist teachers in addressing classroom diversity, preferences in learning style, and different ways of learning and knowing information (Dodge, 2017).

Self-assessment. Another excellent source of student data is student self-assessment. During instruction, teachers should poll students to see where they think they are in their understanding of the lesson, particularly during more complex content instruction (Venables, 2017). To help students feel safe to respond honestly and lessen the pressure to vote as their peers, some teachers employ heads-down voting which involves a show of fingers using the following scale: 1 = Totally confused; 2 = Shaky on this; 3 = I think I get this; and 4 = Got it/let's move on (Venables, 2017).

Self-assessment is part of being a self-regulated learner. Teachers can educate students to be self-regulated by teaching them to self-assess where they are in their learning and set goals as well as how to monitor their own progress (Dyer, 2014). By being able to self-assess, reflect, and react to assessments, students can determine which learning tactics enable them to perform to the best of their abilities (Dyer, 2014).

Mini-presentations. At times, students are able to demonstrate what they are working on or what they have learned, and these can be an additional source of invaluable information for teachers. These presentations allow students to demonstrate their understanding of the content, see and hear content discussed by their peers, and provide a public demonstration of mastery (Venables, 2017).

Having to conduct mini-presentations enables students to own their learning and teach something, giving the content new meaning (Great Schools Partnership, 2014). In preparation for teaching to their classmates, students are able to clarify their own understanding of the material and then act as an instructional resource for their peers. Mini-presentations have the added benefit that knowing they have to perform in front of their teacher and classmates, students will take the assignment more seriously and do better work (Venables, 2017).

Formative data. The collection of formative data prior to an assignment due date can be accomplished through peer evaluation using checklists and rubrics to evaluate the work while it is in progress (Venables, 2017; Dyer, 2014). In this way, students become familiar with the language and expectations within the rubric and students are engaged in conversations about the quality of each other's work (Venables, 2017; Dyer, 2014).

Exit tickets. At the end of each school day, teachers may close their lessons with an exit ticket that contains short reflective questions for students to answer about the content of the day's lessons or how students felt about the material (Venables, 2017). Students may also have solved a problem or summarized their understanding of material presented in class that day (Dodge, 2017).

Exit slips provide teachers with a quick brief check for understanding to see what students really took from class that day (Curran, 2013; Schaaf, 2018). Once data from exit slips is gathered, it may be sorted into groups delineating students who have not yet mastered the skill, students who are ready to apply the skill, and students who are ready to move forward (Venables, 2017; Dodge, 2017).

Once sorted and grouped, teachers may ask students what the next step would be as a result (Dyer, 2014). If students have developed their learning enough to know what comes next, where they are in relation to it, and how to get to that next step, then they have expanded their self-regulatory skills (Curran, 2013). For those that are not ready to move forward and require re-teaching, a needs-based group may be formed so the teacher can review the material using alternative instructional methods (Dodge, 2017).

During collaborative activities, students have an opportunity to communicate with peers as they develop and demonstrate their understanding of the material taught. Listening in on student partners or small-group conversations enables the teacher to quickly identify problems or misconceptions, which can then be addressed in the moment. Group activities should be followed up with an individual activity to more effectively identify each individual student need (Dodge, 2017).

KEEPING TRACK OF AND USING DATA TO IMPROVE INSTRUCTION AND STUDENT LEARNING

One way in which teachers can observe and assess student growth in the classroom is to walk around the room with a clipboard and set of sticky notes. Student names and short comments can be written on each note when the teacher notices the acquisition of a new skill or confusion and struggle with a skill (Lemov, 2015; Dodge, 2017).

Teachers may want to keep a folder for each student to place any notes that may be made so that when conferencing with students it is easier to develop individualized lesson plans (Phillips, 2014). Teachers may also find it helpful to keep track of data using a class list where it can be recorded through a system of check marks (M+, M, M-) or numbers (4, 3, 2, 1) of how the student is doing on specific skills (Dodge, 2017). Regardless of the type of tracking system, educators must find one that works and stick with it (Phillips, 2014).

Teachers should not be afraid of data; rather, it is a puzzle that needs to be broken into its individual pieces and dug into to find useable meaning. The more data sources that teachers examine, the more confident teachers can be moving forward with changes to their instruction that will fulfill the unmet need (Logan, 2017).

Data gathered from formative and summative assessments can be used to communicate with other teachers across all grade levels. Information on what students have learned over the course of an academic year as well as their strengths and weaknesses should be shared with vertical grade-level teams

(Logan, 2017). Sharing information ensures that teachers will be able to plan ahead for individual student needs (Logan, 2017).

Effective feedback is a great way for teachers to use collected data in order to improve student learning (Brookhart, 2017). Teachers are able to create more opportunities to gather data on what students have, and have not learned, and provide effective feedback to students (Brookhart, 2017; Dwyer & William, 2017). Feedback should not be open ended or ambiguous, and teachers should give clear indications of the criteria used to assess the quality of student work. Feedback should be given in a timely manner and based on the criteria accompanying the assignment (Brookhart, 2017).

Dwyer and William (2017) state that there have been valuable and powerful increases in student learning when teachers are able to clearly define the purposes of each lesson, use those lessons to collect evidence on how students learn, and then use the collected data to redirect students as needed. No matter what assessment is used, the results will be beneficial provided they are used in a timely manner to make any necessary adjustments to instruction (Dwyer and William, 2017).

To help improve student learning, teachers should make the expectations clear for each new concept and communicate the criteria for successfully meeting those expectations with the students (Dwyer & William, 2017). Teachers should also provide feedback that clearly and explicitly identify needed improvements in order to move students forward in the learning process and promote students' understanding of concepts (Brookhart, 2017).

Evidence from classroom discussions, student answers, and learning tasks can be used to revise lessons and activities. Teachers can also use a variety of techniques to engage all students in class discussions and use any evidence of student thinking and understanding to plan future instruction (Dwyer & William, 2017). Students should also be encouraged to serve as instructional and learning resources and take responsibility for their own learning (Dwyer & William, 2017).

After reviewing any assessment data, teachers can tier their activities to accommodate two or three levels of learners and provide both corrective activities and enrichment activities for students who need them (Dodge, 2017). Any follow-up, corrective instruction designed to help students must demonstrate concepts in new ways and engage students in different and appropriate learning experiences via changes in format, organization, and/or method of presentation (Dodge, 2017).

Using multiple sources of assessment data to enhance learning outcomes will result in students becoming more engaged with the material and accompanying activities as well as promote action on feedback to improve their assignments (Dwyer & William, 2017; Dodge, 2017). Students will also take responsibility for their own learning and support each other, thus increasing student success. (Dwyer & William, 2017).

FINAL THOUGHTS

Having the means to assess students and their learning provides invaluable information to teachers and school leaders regarding the impact they are having on student learning and success. Formative and summative assessments give the best information possible about a teacher's instructional methods in content areas and can distinguish what is working well and what needs to be modified (Hattie, 2015). Assessment cannot only, and should not only, be used to inform students of their progress in the classroom, rather it should also be used to inform teachers of the influence they have on students' knowledge and achievement within the classroom (Alber, 2017).

Teachers can use data to identify individual student needs, modify curriculum and instruction, identify learning objectives, and recognize individual and group success. Assessment data can also be used by school administrators to supervise teachers, guide discussions, inform teachers of their strengths and weaknesses, and determine if past decisions can be evaluated to see if the desired outcomes were met.

Assessment data also provides students with information on their strengths and weaknesses and can help them become better learners and take more ownership of their learning. Valuable and powerful increases in student learning can be made when teachers clearly define their lessons, assess the effectiveness of the lessons, and then use the collected data in a timely manner to provide for individual students' learning needs.

POINTS TO REMEMBER

- Formative assessments can be used to gather district, school, and grade-level data while individual summative assessments provide educator information on student performance. Used together, multiple means of assessment can provide teachers feedback on classroom instruction and allow them to make modifications to enhance student success.
- Summative assessments are the most frequently used measure of student learning and provide information on an individual student's performance in the classroom. Knowing what a student can do immediately versus what he or she may be able to do later is particularly useful in helping teachers identify learning obstacles and curriculum dysfunction.
- The more data sources that teachers can collect and examine, the more likely they will find a demonstrated unmet need, and the more confident teachers will be in changing their instruction to fulfill that unmet need.
- Corrective instruction, whether it be in format, organization, or method of presentation, must be designed to enhance student learning, knowledge,

and success and must demonstrate concepts in new ways and engage students in different and appropriate learning experiences.
- Using multiple sources of assessment data to enhance learning outcomes will result in more student engagement, students taking responsibility for their own learning, and an increase in student success.

Chapter Eight

Teaching the Whole Child

The Importance of Social-Emotional Learning

Teachers can have a significant impact on student learning in all domains (Yoder, 2014). In addition to the Common Core State Standards, students must be college and career ready when they graduate high school (Dymnicki, Sambolt, & Kidron, 2013). They must possess the skills necessary for appropriate collaboration, self-monitoring of behavior and goal progress, and informed decision-making (CASEL, 2018; Yoder, 2014). Social-emotional learning (SEL) is an excellent way to infuse the academic requirements with the behavioral expectations that all students need so they will be ready for what lies ahead.

Preparing students to be 21st-century learners is at the heart of educational reform, and social-emotional learning is a significant part of the movement. SEL seeks to develop prosocial skills, which supports positive academic outcomes (Espelage, Rose, & Polanin, 2016; Jones & Bouffard, 2012). Through the development of cognitive, interpersonal, and self-esteem strategies, 21st-century students can be nurtured (Pellegrino & Hilton, 2013).

During social-emotional instruction, students acquire competencies that provide a basis for understanding and managing emotions, recognizing and accepting the perspectives of others, developing positive and supportive relationships, and solving conflicts through ethical decision-making (CASEL, 2018, Yoder, 2014). Through the development of these critical skills, teachers create and maintain a safe learning environment that fosters academic and emotional growth and promotes respect, trust, and acceptance (Yoder, 2014).

The Collaborative for Academic, Social, and Emotional Learning (CASEL) (2018) developed five social-emotional competencies meant to promote growth in 21st-century learners. These competencies include development of self-awareness, self-management, social-awareness, relationship management, and responsible decision-making (CASEL, 2018). Research has shown that students' emotional development directly influences motivation, engagement, and relationships both with peers and teachers (Durlak, Dymnicki, Taylor, Weissberg, & Schellinger, 2011).

WHAT IS SOCIAL-EMOTIONAL LEARNING?

SEL involves developing students' social-emotional competencies through knowledge, skills, attitudes, and behaviors (CASEL, 2018; Yoder, 2014). Acquiring these proficiencies allows students to recognize and manage their own emotions, understand and accept the perspectives of others, build and maintain positive relations, solve interpersonal conflicts, and make ethical decisions (Pellegrino & Hilton, 2013; Yoder, 2014).

In order to develop and encourage social-emotional learning, classrooms must embrace a safe and supportive learning environment. The ideal learning environment should foster safety; support academic and emotional development; and be physically welcoming, respectful, trusting, and caring (Yoder, 2014). When referring to a learning environment, the whole school community should be considered, especially where social and emotional development is concerned (Jones & Bouffard, 2012; Yoder, 2014).

Instruction to develop social-emotional skills in students must focus on five interrelated components, which are essential to the cognitive, social, and emotional development of individuals. The five interrelated components include: self-awareness, self-management, social awareness, relationship skills, and responsible decision-making (CASEL, 2018; Espelage et al., 2016).

Self-awareness is the first competency and it allows students to recognize their own feelings, interests, and strengths (CASEL, 2018). When students have the ability to become self-aware, they have an easier time describing and understanding their emotions. This, in turn, can assist with academic choices and performance achievement (CASEL, 2018; Pellegrino & Hilton, 2013; Yoder, 2014).

The second competency, self-management, teaches students how to appropriately handle daily stress and problems and provides strategies to control emotions (CASEL, 2018). Research has proven that emotional stress directly impacts memory and cognitive efforts (Yoder, 2014). When students use self-management strategies, they learn to set goals, monitor their progress, and reflect on their performance. This can directly affect a student's motivation (CASEL, 2018; Yoder, 2014).

Social awareness, the third competency, is the ability to understand and take other perspectives into consideration (Yoder, 2014). This skill is especially important when engaged in collaborative activities, class discussions, and maintaining relationships (CASEL, 2018; Pellegrino & Hilton, 2013). The capacity to understand others' feelings and thoughts can assist students when trying to relate to characters in a text, as an example (Yoder, 2014).

Relationship management is the fourth competency and it helps students to develop and maintain positive peer relationships, resolve interpersonal conflict, resist negative peer pressure, and engage appropriately when working in a cooperative fashion (CASEL, 2018; Yoder, 2014). The last competency, responsible decision-making, encourages students in identifying problems and developing appropriate solutions. When making decisions, students must take into consideration respecting all parties involved, ensuring safety, and making ethical considerations (Pellegrino & Hilton, 2013; Yoder, 2014).

THE IMPORTANCE OF SOCIAL-EMOTIONAL LEARNING

The research on SEL shows a multitude of benefits (Yoder, 2014; CASEL, 2018; Pellegrino & Hilton, 2013). Emotional development directly influences classroom interactions, including, motivation, engagement, and relationships (Pellegrino & Hilton, 2013; Yoder, 2014). The development of social-emotional competencies has proven to increase student motivation, decrease disruptive behaviors, amplify academic achievement, and produce positive social behaviors including improved attitudes toward oneself and others (Yoder, 2014). When examining the benefits of social-emotional learning to academics specifically, students who were exposed to social-emotional learning increased approximately eleven percentile points on standardized tests in comparison to those students with little to no exposure (Durlak et al., 2011).

The skills students develop as a result of social-emotional learning opportunities are critical to meeting the college and career readiness standards of the Common Core State Standards (CCSS). The CCSS requires that students delve deeper into the various content areas and consistently engage in more critical thinking and problem-solving tasks (Yoder, 2014). By developing the social-emotional skills, students are more adept at regulating and managing emotions when tasks are challenging. Displaying negative emotions, such as frustration, drains cognitive resources needed to perform higher-level academic tasks (Durlak et al., 2011; Espelage et al., 2016; Yoder, 2014).

Social-emotional learning skills are critical to navigate the complexity of texts and content that students are exposed to across curricular areas; for example, self-awareness development allows students to notice their strengths and weaknesses (Yoder, 2014). Self-management skills will then encourage students to ask for the help they need through effective communication and interactions with others (Durlak et al., 2011; Yoder, 2014).

MEETING THE FIVE SOCIAL-EMOTIONAL COMPETENCIES

In order for students to fully meet the five competencies for social-emotional learning and development, specific skills can be implemented by the teacher. To develop self-awareness skills, students should label and understand their own emotions, identify their emotional triggers, recognize their strengths as well as weaknesses, and develop self-efficacy skills, which will help boost self-esteem (Espelage et al., 2016).

Self-management skills encompass the ability to set goals and make plans to achieve those goals (Yoder, 2014). Students should also be able to monitor their progress toward achieving their goals, both academically and behaviorally, by regulating their emotions, impulses, and aggressions, managing their stress, advocating for themselves, and using feedback constructively (Yoder, 2014).

The development of social awareness includes being able to identify both verbal and physical social cues from others, understanding the points of view of others, appreciating diversity, and respecting others (Durlak et al., 2011). Students should be able to effectively identify and use resources of family, school, and community to assist them in gaining social awareness (Espelage et al., 2016).

To ensure appropriate relationship development, students should learn to develop effective communication skills in order to make and maintain positive relationships. Further, students will learn how to appropriately manage and express their emotions and resolve conflict. Through the development of these skills, students can then prevent interpersonal conflicts and resist negative social pressures (Yoder, 2014).

Responsible decision-making skills focus on identifying and implementing strategies to effectively problem-solve and base decisions on ethical and responsible information (Pellegrino & Hilton, 2013). Students who are taught to engage in reflective practices, understand that our choices affect future outcomes as well as the people around us (Yoder, 2014).

POSITIVE LEARNING ENVIRONMENTS SUPPORT SOCIAL-EMOTIONAL LEARNING

Schools and teachers can assist in the implementation of SEL by creating and maintaining positive learning environments (Yoder, 2014). Research has identified three overarching themes that support the development of social-emotional learning as engagement, safety, and positive environments (Bridgeland, Bruce, & Hariharan, 2013).

Engagement embodies strong and positive relationships, and students need to feel supported academically and emotionally by their teachers and peers (Yoder, 2014). Safety ensures that students are free from bullying and violence, and feel academically and emotionally safe. To ensure safety, teachers must effectively address any and all behavior problems, so that every student is free to take personal risks (Bridgeland et al., 2013; Yoder, 2014). Positive learning environments work to fulfill the basic student needs including autonomy, competence, and connectedness (Yoder, 2014). Teachers can facilitate this by creating democratic classrooms that offer challenging and relevant learning opportunities (Yoder, 2014).

Administrators can help teachers maintain these environments through relevant professional learning opportunities that focus on developing and encouraging positive learning environments (Bridgeland et al., 2013). Measuring the impact on student achievement is directly related to the learning environment in which these students engage and can be measured using the teacher evaluation system, among other tools (Bridgeland et al., 2013). Administrators can use this evidence to identify areas in which teachers may need additional training and support and then tailor action plans accordingly (Bridgeland et al., 2013).

SUPPORTING TEACHERS TO INCORPORATE SOCIAL-EMOTIONAL LEARNING IN CLASSROOMS

In order to support the implementation of SEL across all classrooms, teachers must have access to systematic supports. School districts should connect social-emotional learning competencies to district initiatives, such as school climate, bullying preventions, and curricular resources (CASEL, 2018). It is also necessary to consistently assess the effectiveness of the program as well as make changes that further improve the learning and supports available (CASEL, 2018; Yoder, 2014).

School administrators can implement specific social-emotional learning programs or integrate SEL into academic learning or curricular materials (CASEL, 2018). Schools should provide teachers with relevant professional development opportunities and consistent support around developing and implementing social-emotional learning competencies. Similar to school district suggestions listed previously, school administrators should connect the social-emotional learning competencies to policies and procedures such as the school vision, mission, and cultural climate (CASEL, 2018; Yoder, 2014).

Teachers can support the implementation of SEL through engagement in specific instructional strategies, assessing the development of the social-emotional learning competencies of their students, and contributing and supporting social-emotional learning initiatives within their schools and districts (CASEL, 2018; Yoder, 2014).

INSTRUCTIONAL PRACTICES THAT MAINTAIN A POSITIVE LEARNING ENVIRONMENT

Research has identified ten SEL instructional strategies that are highly effective ways to create a positive learning environment, including student-centered discipline, teacher language, responsibility and choice, warmth and support, cooperative learning, classroom discussions, self-reflection and self-assessment, balanced instruction, academic press and expectations, and competence building through modeling, practicing, feedback, and coaching (Yoder, 2014; CASEL, 2018).

Student-centered discipline encompasses the use of classroom management strategies that are developmentally appropriate and reasonable (Yoder, 2014). Practices should be proactive and seek to motivate students to succeed. Strategies that offer opportunities for students to be self-directive and held accountable for their choices and actions should be sought out.

To support social-emotional learning in conjunction with student-centered discipline, the RULER approach has been proven highly effective (Yoder, 2014). This approach stands for recognizing, understanding, labeling, expressing, and regulating and focuses on the development of emotional literacy by helping students identify, explain, and understand their emotions (Yoder, 2014).

Teacher language refers to how the teacher speaks to his or her students and consists of more than simply providing praise; rather, it seeks to encourage effort and hard work (Bridgeland et al., 2013). Teachers can assist students in identifying where individual improvement is needed and how to reach academic, social, and/or behavioral goals (Yoder, 2014).

Responsibility and choice refer to the degree to which students can engage in responsible decision-making regarding their work and role as a student (Bridgeland et al., 2013). Positive learning environments seek to offer democratic norms where students have a voice within the classroom community. Classroom norms and rules should be developed with student input, and teachers should ensure that they are developmentally appropriate (Responsive Classroom, 2018; CASEL, 2018).

Responsibility also includes opportunities for students to help and assist others. Teachers can provide occasions for students to help others through peer tutoring, service learning projects, or community service assignments (Yoder, 2014). When students engage in helping others they feel an increased sense of responsibility, which increases their motivation within the learning environment (CASEL, 2018; Responsive Classroom, 2018).

Warmth and support embraces the academic and social encouragement students receive from their teachers and peers (Espelage et al., 2016). Teachers can show support by asking questions, both academic and non-academic, and they can follow up with students after a problem or concern. In addition to engaging students in conversations, teachers can create structures for students to feel included and accepted as well as modeling how to take risks within the learning community (Yoder, 2014).

Cooperative learning is more than students simply working together to complete a task. There are five basic elements embedded in cooperative learning activities, which include positive interdependence, individual accountability, promoting peer success, applying interpersonal and social skills, and group processing (CASEL, 2018). In order to positively impact learning and develop social-emotional competencies, students need to collaboratively process how they work together and monitor their process as a group (Yoder, 2014).

Classroom discussion specifically relates to the conversations that students and teachers have surrounding content and learning (Yoder, 2014). Teachers should ask open-ended questions that allow students to elaborate on their own thoughts and those of others. Students need to learn communication and active listening skills that assist them in building upon other's thoughts and engage in substantive discussions (Yoder, 2014).

Self-reflection and self-assessment involves students actively thinking about and assessing their own work against performance standards (Yoder, 2014). It is important to assist students with ways to identify and improve their performance such as through the use of rubrics, establishing goals, and seeking help and resources (Yoder, 2014).

Balanced instruction incorporates both active and direct instruction as well as individual and cooperative learning activities (Bridgeland et al., 2013). Some learning requires some direct or explicit instruction in order for students to comprehend the information. Active learning opportunities offer meaningful ways for students to engage in the learning process and increase their understanding (Bridgeland et al., 2013). One highly effective method of active learning is known as project-based learning, which incorporates extended periods of student engagement in solving a real-world problem related to the content being taught (Larmer, Mergendoller, & Boss, 2015).

Academic press refers to the teacher's implementation of meaningful and challenging work, while academic expectations refer to the teacher's belief that all students can and will succeed (Yoder, 2014). Teachers can support students through adjusting instruction according to ability levels, providing encouragement when faced with challenging content, and helping to identify and progress toward individual goals.

Competence building through modeling, practicing, feedback, and coaching embeds SEL competencies within the instructional cycle (Pellegrino & Hilton, 2013). The instructional cycle consists of identifying learning goals and objectives, introduction of new material through appropriate instruction and modeling, time for group and individual practice, and the conclusion and reflection of the lesson. It is important that each part of the instructional cycle reinforce one of the five social-emotional learning competencies (CASEL, 2018; Yoder, 2014).

FINAL THOUGHTS

Today's educators are more than just teachers of academics; rather, they must help to develop the whole individual. Although academic performance is paramount, the idea of supporting and nurturing social and emotional growth has increasingly become an important facet of educational reform (Responsive Classroom, 2018; Yoder, 2014). The intent of the Common Core Standards and education in general is to produce students who are not only college and career ready but responsive and respectful global citizens.

In order to achieve this mandate, teachers must ensure that students possess the skills necessary for appropriate collaboration, self-monitoring of behavior and goal progress, and informed decision-making, which can be accomplished through social and emotional teaching (CASEL, 2018; Espelage et al., 2016; Yoder, 2014).

Social and emotional learning embraces the growth of cognitive, interpersonal, and self-esteem development (Pellegrino & Hilton, 2013). During social-emotional instruction, students acquire competencies that allow them to understand their own emotions, recognize the viewpoints of others without judgment, secure positive and supportive relationships, and implement ethical decision-making (CASEL, 2018, Pellegrino & Hilton, 2013; Yoder, 2014).

Five social-emotional competencies for promoting social-emotional growth for our students have been identified (CASEL, 2018). These competencies include the development of self-awareness, self-management, social-awareness, relationship management, and responsible decision-making. Further research has shown that students' emotional development directly influences motivation, engagement, and relationships both with peers and teachers (Durlak et al., 2011; Espelage et al., 2016; Pellegrino & Hilton, 2013).

POINTS TO REMEMBER

- Effective teachers ensure that instruction addresses more than just academics, but also social-emotional development. Through the development of cognitive, interpersonal, and self-esteem development, students develop the skills needed to be responsible and respectful global citizens.
- In order to guarantee the development of the whole individual, teachers must create safe learning environments that foster academic and emotional growth, and promote respect, trust, and acceptance.

- Research has identified five social-emotional competencies that students must develop to become responsible and productive citizens. These competencies include the development of self-awareness, self-management, social awareness, relationship management, and responsible decision-making.
- The development of social-emotional skills promotes positive outcomes for students including increased motivation, engagement, and relationships; equally important, academic achievement is enhanced, disruptive behaviors decrease, and interpersonal skills are nurtured.

Chapter Nine

Potent Administrative Practices

Empowering Teachers to Foster Student Achievement

It is expected that administrators of the 21st century will lead their schools within a framework of collaboration and shared decision-making with educators to support a high level of teaching and learning. This collaborative effort, in addition to effective classroom instruction, leads to school improvement and the ultimate success of students (NASSP & NAESP, 2013; Tek, 2014).

Effective leadership is a catalyst for student learning in that it strengthens professional communities and fosters the use of instructional practices that are associated with scholarly achievement (Mackey, 2016; NASSP & NAESP, 2013). Research has found strong links between leadership and specific administrator behaviors and student achievement, learning, and success (NASSP & NAESP, 2013; Tek, 2014; Mackey, 2016).

Successful leaders are able to shape the school's vision, based on the highest of standards, into one of academic success for all students (Deal & Peterson, 2016). Leadership is not only about organizational improvement, establishing agreed-upon directions for a school, and doing what is needed to support teacher and student success, it is also about knowing what to do, when and how to do it, and why it is being done (NASSP & NAESP, 2013; Deal & Peterson, 2016). Teachers and other school staff should receive support regarding the important part they play in achieving the vision and mission of the school (NASSP & NAESP, 2013).

Chapter 9

THE EMPOWERED TEACHER

With a commitment to teacher growth, leadership, and increased empowerment, the focus of control changes from school administration to the teachers, which directly impacts student success (Gardner-Webb University, 2017). Empowering teachers allows education to change in positive ways as they become the catalyst (Alrubail, 2015). Administrators should consider giving educators the opportunity to become leaders of teaching and learning within the classroom and in the school (Alrubail, 2015).

Providing opportunities and experiences for teachers to grow allows teachers to become more committed to the school's mission and to their own success in the classroom (Deal & Peterson, 2016). When administrators relinquish control to teacher leaders and show trust, teachers become more creative, take more risks, try new approaches to instruction, provide more assistance to students, and are more flexible (Gardner-Webb University, 2017).

By cultivating teacher leadership, administrators can broaden their own reach as leaders and ensure the excellent and equitable public education that all students deserve (Wright, 2016). Administrators should work to intentionally and purposely build leadership capacity to not only improve student achievement, but to retain teachers (Wright, 2016). This can be accomplished through engaging educators in meaningful conversations and encouraging peer observations, co-teaching, and individual professional development (Wright, 2016).

Administrators should listen to teachers and create roles based on student need and teacher expertise; for example, a teacher who is engaged in creating great relationships as a behavior coach may be able to assist others by visiting classrooms and collaborating with student support personnel, such as nurses, school counselors, after-school coordinators, and school psychologists (Hanover Research, 2015). Together they are able to view the school's, and individual student's, behavior data to give teachers and administrators more time to focus on instruction (Wright, 2016).

Administrators can demonstrate respect for educators and the part they play in creating a healthy learning community atmosphere where hard work is required, students are central, and successes are shared and celebrated (Wright, 2016). Equally important, administrators can set the tone for a school's culture by hanging framed pictures of students and families in the hallways and placing the school's mission and vision in strategic places throughout the school (Wright, 2016).

Leaders who seek to empower teachers are able to effectively and clearly define their vision, filter mandates, and present expectations in alignment with their vision (Deal & Peterson, 2016). Great leaders know which messages to bring forward and are experts at aligning new ideas, mandates, and programs with their vision and promoting these ideas to teachers (Godbold, 2013). Framing every mandate in alignment with the vision allows school leaders to further support one central message that teachers are continually empowered to work toward (Godbold, 2013; Deal & Peterson, 2016).

Teachers should be encouraged to seek professional partnerships and relationships beyond their building, and time spent in activities outside of school should be modeled, supported, and promoted by the administration (Godbold, 2013). Collaboration with others outside of teaching can foster new ideas and ways of thinking that are above and beyond what one mind alone can conceive (Godbold, 2013).

Teachers who would like to take on leadership roles should have a clear definition of great teaching and be forward thinking in their beliefs, goals, and objectives (Center for Teaching Quality, National Board for Professional Standards, and the National Education Association, 2014). Teacher leaders should be proactive in their personal and professional development and willing to share any learned information, strategies, and success stories with their colleagues (Schwartz, 2016).

Administrators who seek to empower teachers must provide clear paths and directions on how to explore problems and devise solutions (Schwartz, 2016). To facilitate a shift from problems and complaints to solutions and help, administrators may want to consider putting rules in place, such as for every problem that needs to be discussed, two potential solutions should be arrived at before collaborative problem solving can take place (Godbold, 2013). Effective leaders not only establish procedures for exploring problems but also provide relevant resources for professional and personal development (Center for Teaching Quality, National Board for Professional Standards, and the National Education Association, 2014).

Teacher leaders begin the process of empowerment by making the conscious decision to embrace the power to live and teach on their terms (Godbold, 2013). Empowered teachers also know and can articulate their beliefs about what makes great teaching (Center for Teaching Quality, National Board for Professional Standards, and the National Education Association, 2014). They decide what to embrace, how to incorporate it into their teaching style, what to leave out, and what they have to do in order to work collaboratively with other professionals (Godbold, 2013).

In terms of professional development and collaboration, empowered teachers bring more to the table than just knowledge; they bring passion, interests, curiosity, adventure, relationships and a variety of experiences (Schwartz, 2016). Teachers should actively seek to develop themselves personally as they attempt to authentically reach students. Empowered educators know that to articulate and act upon professional beliefs, they must consistently work on becoming better teachers themselves; they are not only rewarded by administrators, they are rewarded by seeing growth and success in students (Godbold, 2013).

SUPPORTIVE RELATIONSHIPS BETWEEN ADMINISTRATORS AND TEACHERS

One of the main duties of a school administrator is to provide teachers with ongoing, collaborative support. Relationships should be cultivated slowly, taking enough time to get to know each teacher's strength and weaknesses (Meador, 2017c). Effective administrators initially make small changes that allow teachers time to get to know them, followed by larger, more meaningful changes over time. Significant changes should be made only after seeking and considering input from teachers (Meador, 2017c).

Providing effective teacher support requires fair and consistent decision making, meaningful evaluations, and oftentimes constructive criticism and praise (Meador, 2017e). To have meaning, evaluations should be conducted through collaborative information gathering over the course of many visits to the classroom and contain a balance of praise and helpful criticism (Meador, 2017e). Administrators should provide 100 percent support to their teachers as long as they believe they are effective, ethical, and moral (Edwards & Hinueber, 2015).

Administrators should know each teacher's individual strengths and weaknesses and develop a plan with him or her to provide assistance that focuses on the needed areas of improvement through the use of resources, suggestions, and professional development opportunities (Meador, 2017d). In developing such plans, the focus should be narrowed to the area requiring the most improvement and when that area is sufficiently improved upon, move on to the next area (Meador, 2017d).

It is critical that teachers understand that administrators are genuinely trying to help them throughout this process and that they have the teachers' best interests in mind. Strong administrators should build relationships with teachers that allow them to be critical when necessary without hurting a teacher's feelings (Meador, 2007e). Building relationships of trust is a balancing act of professional and personal interest. Administrators should take an active role understanding and supporting teachers' families, hobbies, and interests, being careful not to get so close that they cannot make a tough decision when necessary. Showing an active interest in a teacher's life outside the classroom will demonstrate that administrators care about teachers as individuals and not just as educators (Meador, 2017e).

To develop and maintain strong relationships with teachers, administrators should adhere to an open-door policy. This allows teachers the safety to bring any problem or issue forward and trust that administrators will help them while keeping information confidential (Meador, 2017e). Sometimes teachers need someone to listen while they vent about their frustrations, and having good listening skills is essential. Administrators should not force their opinions on teachers; rather, they should offer options and explanations from their perspective and state what decisions would be made and why, keeping in mind that every situation is unique (Edwards & Hinueber, 2015).

Administrators should offer advice, direction, or assistance to teachers at all levels of experience but in particular to new and inexperienced teachers (Meador, 2017e). Assistance can be as simple as having a teacher observe another teacher whose strengths are in an area where that teacher needs assistance or providing books and resources for the teacher to use as they need (Hanover Research, 2015).

Administrators should model a lesson that focuses on an individual teacher's weakness and then teach that lesson to the teacher's class. Teachers are able to observe how to do things the right way, make notes on it, and gain an understanding of what they need to change and how to do it (Edwards & Hinueber, 2015). Administrators are then able to follow up with the teacher and have a conversation that focuses on how the teacher can improve based on what was observed (Meador, 2017d).

It is good practice for experienced teachers to become mentors to less experienced teachers, thus sharing insights and experiences. Every teacher should be given the opportunity to observe an established veteran teacher (Meador, 2017d). Given time to work together in a collaborative effort, teachers will strengthen relationships and provide less experienced teachers with best practices, success stories, and struggles/solutions (Meador, 2017d).

Struggling teachers should also be given a variety of resources that include multiple strategies for improvement such as books, articles, videos, and websites. After they have had time to go over the material, administrators should follow up with conversations to see what the teachers were able to gain from the resources as well as how they plan to incorporate it into the classroom (Meador, 2017e).

Administrative Observation and Recognition

One of the major components of a school administrator's job is to improve teacher quality. Effective school leaders have the ability to assist an ineffective educator—moving them from "needs improvement" to "proficient" and then to "exemplary" (Massachusetts Department of Education, 2017). Observations with actionable feedback are the single most critical aspect to improve the quality of a teacher. School administrators should routinely observe and evaluate a teacher's classroom to identify areas of need and weakness and to create an individual plan for improvement (Massachusetts Department of Education, 2017).

School leaders should encourage inexperienced or struggling teachers to keep a journal to provide insight and understanding. Through journaling, teachers can grow and improve through reflection as well as recognize individual strengths and weaknesses. Journals can also serve as a reminder of what worked and what did not in the classroom (Meador, 2017d). Teachers are able to look back at where they were and see how much growth has occurred over time (Meador, 2017d).

Video recording a series of classroom lessons may also be advantageous to educators in that they can watch themselves and understand what administrators or mentors see (Scott, 2013). When given the opportunity to observe themselves, teachers are able to have powerful reflections and realize what they may need to change in their approach to teaching (Scott, 2013).

To enable continued growth and empowerment, administrators need to recognize teachers, their efforts, and their professional accomplishments, yet, due to shrinking school budgets, administrators are finding it increasingly difficult to provide significant opportunities to motivate and inspire teachers (Gardner-Webb University, 2017; Education World, 2017). To reassure teachers they are working to their potential and beyond, administrators can recognize teachers' efforts and contributions by offering both public and private positive feedback through weekly memos, emails, and regular staff meetings (Levin & Schrum, 2017).

Administrators are also encouraged to make unscheduled observations of teachers at least two times per month and take a moment to scribble a positive comment on a sticky note that can be left on the teacher's desk before moving on to the next classroom (Levin & Schrum, 2017). It is also important to ensure that every teacher has the chance to visit another classroom during the year to watch and learn, ask questions, and see best practices in action (Levin & Schrum, 2017).

Effective Communication and Collaboration

To effect systemic change and implement large-scale initiatives, such as the Common Core State Standards, which requires rethinking professional learning, curriculum and instructional materials, family and community engagement, and assessment of the education system, collaboration is essential (O'Brien, 2014). Research has demonstrated that collaboration does not work if school leaders do not put a vast amount of work, planning, and trust into it (Inclusive Schools Network, 2015).

To improve education, educators and administrators should place an emphasis on teacher quality, including professional development, new systems of evaluation, peer-to-peer assistance and mentoring programs (O'Brien, 2014). Teachers and administrators should work collaboratively to undergo substantive problem-solving, discover new means of innovation, and pursue new avenues of experimentation to address critical issues (O'Brien, 2014).

Collaboration should include a review of any gathered data and input from teachers and other staff to outline or modify the school's action plan (Inclusive Schools Network, 2015). Everyone should be working from the same knowledge base and administrators should never assume that all teachers have the same levels of learning regarding teaching strategies and best practices (Inclusive Schools Network, 2015).

Collaborative structures with an infrastructure that promotes and facilitates collaborative decision-making through leadership teams, school improvement committees, and school advisory councils that meet regularly play a key role in school decision-making (O'Brien, 2014). Monthly meetings for teachers, teacher leaders, and administrators will help support teachers in their effort to attain student success and attain the skills needed for schools to succeed.

This system of collaboration also offers educators a conducive and free-flowing environment to bring forward, discuss, and address any concerns they may have (O'Brien, 2014). Administrators and teachers should strive to attend school board meetings and parent information sessions together and speak with one unified voice (O'Brien, 2014).

School leaders should maintain an open-door policy where teachers are encouraged to discuss concerns or seek advice through ongoing and continuous dynamic dialogue (Watkins, 2016). To improve teacher quality and see growth, it is essential that administrators build engaging, trusting relationships with teachers. To be effective, school leaders must be active listeners, offer encouragement, and constructive criticism and suggestions when appropriate (Meador, 2017c).

Administrators can benefit from in-depth, regularly scheduled conversations with their teachers about classroom occurrences and activities as well (Watkins, 2016). Informal, open, and honest conversations not only give administrators perspective about what is happening in the classroom, they enable administrators to provide teachers with helpful suggestions and tips (Meador, 2017c). Active listening will also build trust between administrators and teachers and can lead to helpful conversations that will significantly improve teacher effectiveness (Meador, 2017f).

Administrators should foster the trust relationship by creating a trusting, encouraging atmosphere where all teachers are able to communicate and collaborate. To ensure positive learning experiences, ongoing daily mentoring relationships can be developed in which both parties have similar personalities (Watkins, 2016). Experienced veteran teachers can provide tremendous insight and encouragement, as well as share best practices with an inexperienced or struggling teacher (Meador, 2017f).

School environments themselves must support collaboration, team building, and the creation of a positive culture, whether it be through teacher lunches, day trips, and/or coffee chats before class (Alrubail, 2015). An emphasis on communication will also help build a positive school culture. When teachers are empowered to express thoughts and ideas in a safe and positive environment, this mind-set will extend into the classroom (Alrubail, 2015; Watkins, 2016).

It is also essential that teachers are provided with individualized support. Literacy or math coaches can model lessons, observe classes, and provide constructive feedback to teachers (Center for Comprehensive School Reform and Management, 2017). Appropriate modeling can also provide teachers, particularly new teachers, with the benefit of peer observations, debriefing sessions with colleagues, and appropriate constructive feedback (Center for Comprehensive School Reform and Management, 2017).

School leaders should separate feedback into two distinct processes so that teachers will not be afraid of taking the risk to try something new in their classroom. Evaluation systems should reward and recognize teachers for their performance while providing consequences for poor performance, but also provide developmental feedback to help them improve, without any negative repercussions (Massachusetts Department of Education, 2017; Roscorla, 2017).

Principals and other administrators can play a significant role in helping educators teach effectively and promote student success (Roscorla, 2017). School districts can create opportunities for teachers and administrators to work together to analyze student performance and identify and concentrate on priority areas for improvement (O'Brien, 2014). Inclusive cultures that provide opportunities for involvement, communication, collaboration, and respect for teachers as professionals is essential for not only the success of administrators and teachers, but the students as well (O'Brien, 2014).

School leaders need to provide teachers with myriad resources that enable students to learn independently and in small groups. By providing laptops, bandwidth, and software subscriptions, teachers will have more time to work with students one-on-one or in small groups as needed while the other students perform work online and collaborate on assignments (Roscorla, 2017). When principals mentor and coach teachers, they not only build teacher confidence, but also present ideas on how to improve student success and confidence (Roscorla, 2017).

Shared Decision-Making

Research suggests that leaders who set a clear sense of direction and are invested in developing people and fostering relationships have the greatest impact and are the most successful (Center for Comprehensive School Reform and Management, 2017). The development of a shared understanding of the school and its goals becomes the basis for a sense of purpose and vision and assists teachers in making sense of their work while enabling them to find a sense of identity within their work context (DeMatthews, 2014; Lin, 2014).

To provide effective direction, administrators should have an understanding of direction setting and the amount of time required to develop a shared understanding of what the school should look like and what needs to be done to achieve that (DeMatthews, 2014). Administrators should recognize and know that including teachers and other staff in identifying goals will make teachers more motivated to achieve school, as well as individual, goals and visions (Lin, 2014).

Teachers who are given the opportunity to engage in open and honest communication with their administration, contribute their suggestions, and voice their concerns are more likely to follow the direction set by the administration (Center for Comprehensive School Reform and Management, 2017). Although administrators, particularly principals, are the primary decision makers, school administration should provide teachers with the opportunity to participate in regularly scheduled meetings and committees that are involved in decision-making on school policies and goals, change implementations, strategies, deadlines, and logistics (Alrubail, 2015, DeMatthews, 2014).

Educators should be empowered with the right to exercise professional judgment on what and how to teach, and support should be given to teacher initiatives and ideas regarding professional development (Alrubail, 2015; Gardner-Webb University, 2017; Education World, 2017). Teachers should also be permitted the opportunity and means to express their feelings and provide advice, particularly when any issues, such as curriculum development and design, directly affect the teachers (Alrubail 2015; Lin, 2014).

Professional Development

Administrators must provide experiences for teachers to grow as leaders, and although school funds are dwindling for some, providing professional development opportunities is essential (Gardner-Webb University, 2017, Meador, 2017b). Opportunities for professional growth and development provide teachers the opportunity to accept leadership roles and participation in these roles enables teachers to learn new skills to increase student learning. (Rizvi, 2016; Hanover Research, 2012).

Teachers should always be encouraged to seek out professional development courses or workshops. Participation in professional development opportunities in which teachers can learn from other teachers and have more time to collaborate will lead to teacher empowerment and an increase in productivity (Rizvi, 2016). Topics for development can include teaching ways of thinking, or mind-sets, that foster creativity, a passion for learning, teacher growth, and the ability to take ownership of learning (Roscorla, 2017). Collaborative experiences during staff meetings and professional development days allow teachers to share ideas they have learned and discuss student performance, curriculum, and instruction as well as provide encouragement and support (Hanover Research, 2012; Education World, 2017).

Participation is required in professional development, and teachers want professional development opportunities that are applicable to their situations. Administrators should choose opportunities that will benefit teachers, not just those that meet minimum professional development criteria (Meador, 2017b). Teachers should be given professional development opportunities that are unique to their own individual needs in which they can gain valuable, applicable insights for immediate application in their classroom (Rizvi, 2016). Engaging professional development can motivate, provide innovative ideas, and give a fresh perspective from an outside source (Hanover Research, 2012).

As many teachers may have limited experience with educational theories and student questioning techniques, it is imperative that schools target appropriate professional development opportunities that will improve and enhance the good teaching practices already in place and provide information about other effective learning strategies that may be used (Inclusive Schools Network, 2015). Book studies, PLCs, professional development sessions, conferences, or visits to high-performing schools are all valuable means to provide intellectual stimulation and valuable learning experiences (Center for Comprehensive School Reform and Management, 2017).

The Role of Administration in Student Success

To provide successful guidance to teachers, administrators should be tuned in to their own emotional intelligence as well as their ability and willingness to be aware of teachers not only as employees, but also as individuals (Center for Comprehensive School Reform and Management, 2017). Administrators should not be afraid to pay personal attention to a teacher and through the utilization of the teacher's capabilities, increase enthusiasm and optimism, which will then reduce frustration, transmit a sense of mission, and increase performance (Center for Comprehensive School Reform and Management, 2017).

Administrators play a key role in the delivery of quality instruction within their school. Responsibilities include ensuring educational strategies are in place that support effective learning for all students and facilitating, guiding, and supporting quality instructional practices. Effective administrators understand that improved test scores are important but know that quality instruction is essential for improving student achievement (Inclusive Schools Network, 2015).

It is imperative that school administrators have a working knowledge of effective instructional strategies and understand the needs of students and teachers. It is essential that they understand that effective teaching strategies are appropriate for all students whether they have been identified as requiring support through 504, Response to Intervention (RTI), Special Education eligibility, or state assessments results (RTI Action Network, 2018).

Current practices should be reviewed on an annual basis to determine if they have been successful, whether the practices have been used with fidelity, monitoring of implementation has taken place, and student achievement has been positively impacted (RTI Action Network, 2018). After determining which practices have been effective, the information should be shared with teachers to ensure the strategies are incorporated in their teaching practices. In the meantime, ongoing professional development and monitoring of teacher implementation should continue (Inclusive Schools Network, 2015; RTI Action Network, 2018).

FINAL THOUGHTS

Educational administrators are considered the most influential leaders, and their guidance is intricately linked to student performance and success. Successful administration, collaboration, and effective classroom instruction can lead to school improvement and the ultimate success of students. Administrative efforts to provide teachers with opportunities and experiences to grow result in a stronger commitment to the school's mission and to their own success in the classroom. Professional growth and development opportunities provide teachers the resources they will need to accept leadership roles, learn new skills, and increase student learning.

Teachers should be provided with the opportunity to participate in decisions on school policies and goals, school change, and strategies. Educators should also be empowered with the right to exercise professional judgment on teaching and be supported on teacher initiatives, curriculum development and design, and ideas regarding professional development.

Collaboration is essential to the implementation of large-scale initiatives and the identification of effective practices. Shared decision-making through leadership teams and school committees will help support teachers as they strive for improved student outcomes, while ongoing, collaborative support, fair and consistent decision-making by administrators, and meaningful evaluations will build strong, trusting relationships that will further a positive and successful learning environment.

Participation in school-wide decision-making and professional development opportunities leads to teacher empowerment and an increase in productivity. Administrators should choose opportunities that will benefit teachers and that are unique to their individual needs so they are able to gain valuable skills and insights that can be used immediately in their classroom. Teacher engagement in professional development opportunities will motivate, provide innovative ideas, and lead to student success.

POINTS TO REMEMBER

- Positive school change occurs with the empowerment of teachers. Administrative commitment to teacher growth and leadership will directly impact student success.
- Building leadership capacity through meaningful conversations, actionable feedback, and professional development will improve student achievement and teacher retention.
- By adhering to an open-door policy where teachers can confidentially, and without judgment, bring any issue forward, administrators are able to build strong, safe, and trusting relationships with teachers.
- School administrators must assist ineffective teachers as they move from "needs improvement" to "proficient" and beyond through collaboration, active-listening, shared decision-making, meaningful evaluations, and teacher empowerment.

Chapter Ten

Integrating Technology, Teaching, and Learning

Changing with the Times

Twenty-first-century teaching and learning demands the use of technology supports through the use of digital learning tools, 24/7 open access, personalized learning opportunities, and increased student engagement and motivation (U.S. Department of Education, 2017). Technology can supplement typical classroom instruction by providing authentic learning opportunities, activities for cooperative learning, and supports for various learning styles (U.S. Department of Education, 2017).

Technology offers students and educators digital learning tools, flexible support, and expanded communication opportunities for all students (U.S. Department of Education, 2017). Technology can also support and maintain learning communities outside of the physical school building, which helps to develop lifelong learners and digitally responsible citizens (Wistrom, 2015). There are many ways to incorporate technology into the learning process, such as blended learning, flipped classroom, embedded support, and online learning (U.S. Department of Education, 2017).

The U.S. Department of Education (2017), National Education Technology Plan Update set a vision for learning enabled through the incorporation of technology. The plan is comprised of five over-overarching themes that support many critical components (U.S. Department of Education, 2017). The first theme is learning—that is, creating a vision of what students need to know and understand as well as how to bring equity to the learning space.

The second theme is teaching, and here the focus is on the roles and practices of educators (U.S. Department of Education, 2017). Leadership is the third theme, and this sets the vision, discusses budgeting, and focuses on implementation. Within the theme of assessment, the plan provides a pathway to transform assessment to be technology based and also ensures that resources and connectivity are secured (U.S. Department of Education, 2017). The last theme is infrastructure, and this theme is responsible for ensuring access and effective use (U.S. Department of Education, 2017).

A meta-analysis of research on technology integration to support teaching and learning revealed that the benefits included the increased opportunities for personalized learning, engagement in real-world challenges, expansion of the learning environment to extend outside the confines of a school building, and meeting the needs of diverse student populations (U.S. Department of Education, 2017).

Through the use of technology, students can learn how to be responsible digital citizens and reach the college and career readiness standards of the Common Core (Wistrom, 2015). With the assistance of technology, students learn how to think critically, solve complex problems, participate in collaborative activities appropriately, and boost self-belief and confidence (U.S. Department of Education, 2017).

Technology also supports the development of non-cognitive competencies and having a growth mind-set, which are equally as important as academic skills (Durlak et al., 2011; Dweck, 2007). Non-cognitive skills encompass such things as successfully navigating challenging tasks, developing and maintaining relationships, solving everyday problems, and developing self-awareness (Durlak et al., 2011).

THE BENEFITS OF TECHNOLOGY USE IN EDUCATION

The use of technology has urged educators to rethink how and where students learn (McKnight et al., 2016). Up until now, learning has been confined to resources within a school building. With technology, the walls within our classrooms have come down and learning can now occur anywhere. Through the use of digital devices, students are able to gain knowledge, tap into resources, and connect with others around the world (U.S. Department of Education, 2017).

Technology can be used to adapt instruction and provide accessibility to meet the needs of all students (McKnight et al., 2016). Through the incorporation of technology, teachers can accommodate and strengthen new and expanded student relationships with other peers, teachers, and mentors (U.S. Department of Education, 2017). Learning opportunities with technology expand academic growth possibilities.

The U.S. Department of Education (2017) conducted a meta-analysis of the research on technology and student achievement and summarized the following benefits of instruction enhanced by technology. First, technology enables teachers to personalize learning and educational experiences, giving students myriad choices so that they are more engaged and motivated during the learning process (U.S. Department of Education, 2017).

Secondly, technology assists with the organization of learning and offers real-world challenges (U.S. Department of Education, 2017). One way that teachers can support this is through the implementation of project-based learning activities. Project-based learning provides students with authentic real-world problems while developing 21st-century skills through engaged creativity (Larmer, Mergendoller, & Boss, 2015).

Technology allows teachers and students to move outside of the confines of classroom walls and into learning environments that have no time or space boundaries, thus creating further opportunities for shared educational experiences (U.S. Department of Education, 2017; Larmer et al., 2015). The fourth finding supports the need for students to pursue personal interests through access to technology. When students pursue their passions, they are practicing exploration research and developing lifelong-learning skills (Larmer et al., 2015; U.S. Department of Education, 2017).

The final theme exposed in their research revealed that through technology, transformative learning opportunities are available for all students (U.S. Department of Education, 2017). Access to technology contributes to the equitable divide of educational resources, as students are provided and exposed to appropriate digital resources and pacing based upon their individual learning needs (U.S. Department of Education, 2017).

Technology and Student Achievement

Technology offers a powerful tool to transform teaching and learning. Through technology, collaboration is supported, accessibility is enhanced, learning experiences become authentic, and equity becomes the norm (McKnight et al., 2015; U.S. Department of Education, 2017). Technology is beneficial for personalizing learning opportunities for all students, as teachers can provide students with various choices including what they learn, how they learn, and the pace at which they learn (McKnight et al., 2015).

COLLEGE AND CAREER READINESS AND 21ST-CENTURY SKILLS DEVELOPMENT

The Common Core State Standards ensure that students will be college and career ready by the time they graduate from high school. Part of being college and career ready is becoming an engaged and responsible digital citizen within the global economy (Wistrom, 2015; Huseman, 2015). To become an engaged and responsible citizen, students must learn to think critically, solve complex problems, participate in collaborative activities, and develop self-belief and confidence (Burns, 2015; Huseman, 2015).

In addition to academic achievement, digital citizens must possess non-cognitive skills, have a growth mind-set, and be connected to learning opportunities. Digital citizens develop the skills to use technology in meaningful ways, productive ways, and in safe and respectful environments (Burns, 2015; Wistrom, 2015).

Using Technology to Develop Non-Cognitive Competencies

Having a growth mind-set is critical for succeeding in life and in society. Having a growth mind-set means understanding that a person's abilities can be developed through effort and practice, which leads to increased motivation and personal achievement (Dweck, 2007; Durlak et al., 2011). Developing a growth mind-set requires the promotion of non-cognitive skills.

Non-cognitive competencies are just as important as academic competencies when reaching college and career readiness (Durlak et al., 2011). Non-cognitive competencies include skills such as being able to successfully navigate challenging tasks, form and maintain relationships, solve everyday problems, develop self-awareness, control impulsivity, work cooperatively with others, and care about oneself and others (Durlak et al., 2011; Farrington et al., 2012).

Through the use of technology, non-cognitive skills can be developed. Engagement in digital game simulations, for example, offers students a chance to practice various responses and gauge outcomes to situations. Students can rehearse how to handle conflicts, resolve disputes, and persist through challenges (Farrington et al., 2012). Virtual learning environments can also help to increase empathy, self-awareness, emotional regulation, social awareness, cooperation, and problem-solving skills (U.S. Department of Education, 2017).

TEACHING WITH TECHNOLOGY

The incorporation of technology into the classroom environment creates a learning community that can be supported outside of the physical classroom (McKnight et al., 2015). When using technology to support and engage students, the role of the teacher becomes more of a facilitator or guide through the learning process (Morrison, 2014). By taking on this new role, teachers are able to collaborate alongside their students and push students to dive deeper into the content.

Flipped Classrooms and Flipped Learning

Flipped learning is an instructional strategy that focuses on supporting students in applying knowledge and achieving learning objectives through more in-depth learning (Brame, 2013). Rather than direct instruction occurring in the classroom by the teacher, students gain background knowledge outside of school, as homework, and come to class to engage in deep discussions and collaborative activities (Brame, 2013).

Flipped learning has increased in popularity for several reasons. First, the use of multimedia technology to support and individualize student learning and broaden the learning environment are critical for developing active learners (Francl, 2014). The availability of videos and resources prior to coming to class allows students the opportunities to gain meaningful background knowledge. This second reason allows students with newly acquired schema to engage in higher-level activities, which support deeper learning (Lasry, Dugdale, & Charles, 2014).

Myriad digital teaching resources that are easy to save, revise, and manage are the third reason, and they make teaching and learning more productive (Francl, 2014; Lasry, et al., 2014). Fourth, the in-class activities support collaboration between peers and teachers, which addresses social and emotional development (CASEL, 2018). Similarly, active learning cooperative activities increase student engagement and motivation (Francl, 2014; Lasry, et al., 2014). Finally, flipped learning encourages the use of instructional strategies such as project-based learning and problem-based learning, which support higher-order thinking skills (Francl, 2014; Lasry, et al., 2014).

In flipped classrooms, teachers provide students with videos, lectures, and links to websites, which students watch and explore at home to form basic knowledge and understanding (Brame, 2013). This is referred to as self-learning (Kumon, 2015). Students then come to class prepared to fully engage in applying, transferring, and evaluating their learning in real-world tasks alongside their peers and teacher (Brame, 2013).

Hwang, Lai, and Wang (2015) conducted a study examining the benefits of flipped classrooms and identified several positive attributes including innovative and effective instructional approaches for all students. Implementing flipped learning takes learning from a teacher-centered approach to a student-centered approach, which meets the needs of a diverse set of students. Another benefit was that switching in-class instruction time to at-home practice time allows for more in-depth learning to occur (Hwang et al., 2015).

Characteristics of a flipped classroom include such things as changes in class time, homework expectations, student and teacher interactions, and the involvement of technology (Brame, 2013). Class time is devoted to discussions, projects, problem solving, and applying new knowledge, while teachers create and identify videos and other digital aspects for students to access outside of school (Brame, 2013; Abeysekera & Dawson, 2014).

Interactions between students and teacher are supported through problem solving and collaborative activities focused on applying, analyzing, and evaluating new information. Finally, flipped classrooms are highly engaged in supporting the use of technology to present information to students and in assisting teachers in creating digitally created materials and activities (Abeysekera & Dawson, 2014).

Blended Learning Opportunities

Blended learning incorporates both face-to-face learning opportunities and online integration (U.S. Department of Education, 2017). Blended learning has many positive attributes including being able to accommodate various learning styles and abilities; improving student productivity; accelerating learning; decreasing the cost of instructional materials; and taking advantage of learning opportunities outside of the physical classroom (Tucker, 2013).

Open Education Resources

Open educational resources are comprised of teaching, learning, and research sources freely available in the public domain (U.S. Department of Education, 2017). Teachers and students can access websites, podcasts, digital libraries and portfolios, learning games, and digital textbooks to name a few. Open educational resources provide accessibility for all students, allowing individualized learning and pacing (U.S. Department of Education, 2017).

Universal Design for Learning

Accessibility for all learners is a critical component of any technology used for learning, and many accessibility features are built into software. Similarly, the use of Universal Design for Learning (UDL) is a proactive way to incorporate technology and supports into the learning environment for all students (CAST, 2018). UDL is a framework developed through the fields of neuroscience and education to identify the best strategies to support the way individuals learn (CAST, 2018). UDL embraces three principles aligned with the networks within the brain that are responsible for learning: the affective, the recognition, and the strategic networks (CAST, 2018).

The three principles within the UDL framework include: multiple means of representation, multiple means of expression, and multiple means of engagement (CAST, 2018). Multiple means of representation refers to ways in which teachers present information to their students. When incorporating technology, teachers can use digital books, videos, websites, screen readers, text-to-speech, adjusted reading levels, and translation software to help students comprehend new content (U.S. Department of Education, 2017).

Having multiple means of expression supports choices in the ways in which students demonstrate their comprehension. Students are provided with options for displaying output. Technology can support this through speech-to-text software, online concept mapping, creation of slideshows, podcasts, or blogs to name a few (Archer & Hughes, 2011; U.S. Department of Education, 2017).

With multiple means of engagement teachers can identify and support learning activities that ensure students will be engaged, interested, and offered options (U.S. Department of Education, 2017). Technology can accelerate this through the use of online collaboration tools and, in addition, students should be offered the choice to work collaboratively or alone (CAST, 2018; Archer & Hughes, 2011). Engagement also supports the need to relate topics and information to the interests of the students so that they feel the work is relevant and meaningful.

FINAL THOUGHTS

Through the use of technology, students have access to 24/7 learning opportunities. The constrictive walls of the classroom come down and allow learning to occur anywhere. The integration of digital tools in the learning environment provides students personalized learning opportunities and increases student engagement and motivation. Technology supports authentic learning and collaboration, and accommodates a wide range of learning styles and abilities (U.S. Department of Education, 2017).

Through technology, students receive the tools they need to become active lifelong learners and responsible digital citizens and to expand communication opportunities through learning communities within and outside the classroom (Durlak et al., 2011; U.S. Department of Education, 2017). Technology can be incorporated through many avenues, including blended learning opportunities, flipped classrooms, and supplemental resources (Brame, 2013; Tucker, 2013).

The U.S. Department of Education (2017) National Education Technology Plan (NETP) sets a vision for learning enabled through the incorporation of technology. Included in the plan are three umbrella components that set the stage for technology incorporation, including leadership, setting the vision for how technology will be incorporated throughout the learning process; teaching, taking the vision and implementing it within the classroom; and assessment (U.S. Department of Education, 2017).

Research has proven the vast benefits to students and teachers through the use of technology. Positive outcomes from technology integration include individualized learning opportunities through tailoring instruction based upon student interest and learning styles, engagement in real-world problem solving, and collaborative learning occasions (U.S. Department of Education, 2017). These outcomes directly correlate to the intent of the Common Core Standards, which is to have all students college and career ready by high school graduation (Durlak et al., 2011; Huseman, 2015).

POINTS TO REMEMBER

- Through the integration of technology, students can engage in learning opportunities both within and outside of the school setting. Technology supports the development of active lifelong learning for all individuals.
- Three overarching themes are critical to the overall support of incorporation of technology into teaching and learning. These themes are administrative support, teacher carryout, and assessment data collection and review.
- With the help of technology, teachers can encourage and support academic and social growth through expanded relationships and connections, personalized learning, and engagement in real-world problem solving.
- Non-cognitive skills are just as important as academic skills and achievement and support a growth mind-set and include successful navigation of challenges including perseverance, sustaining positive relationships, gaining self-confidence in one's abilities, and working collaboratively.

Chapter Eleven

Making Professional Development Meaningful

Promising Approaches and Practices

Professional development is any ongoing training and learning experience that cultivates skills, knowledge, and/or dispositions while deepening teaching practices (Yaron, 2017). Through adequate training, teachers are able to improve in areas of deficiency, gain new knowledge or insight into a particular area, or be refreshed in a specific area as needed (Meador, 2017b).

Effective professional development should not be a one-shot deal consisting of disconnected workshops and mundane PowerPoints that tell teachers what they already know (Morrison, 2015). Bringing teachers together for the sake of a meeting to disseminate information that could have been emailed is an example of professional development that will only serve to further any disconnect from classroom realities (Yaron, 2017). Ineffective professional development is detrimental as it devalues the time of teachers who already do not have enough time and does not promote teacher investment (Yaron, 2017).

Quality professional development should represent the height of teaching by being purposeful, relevant, and differentiated (Darling-Hammond, Hyler, & Gardner, 2017). People should be brought together to fulfill a vision of what schools and districts can, and should, be. Professional development, done correctly, has the power to meaningfully enhance teaching and learning practices and transform the culture of a school or district (Morrison, 2015; Yaron, 2017).

EFFECTIVE PROFESSIONAL DEVELOPMENT

Educational staff development is essential for producing highly qualified teachers that must meet the state and federal teacher standards of competency established by the federal Department of Education in their *No Child Left Behind* (NCLB) legislation, further delineated by the Every Student Succeeds Act of 2015 (ESSA) and the National Board for Professional Teaching Standards (NBPTS) (Center for Parent Information & Resources, 2017; Klein, 2015; Brown, 2016). With effective professional development taught by leading teachers in the field, other teachers will be more effective and competent in teaching subject matter, teaching methods, and interaction with students (ASCD, 2017).

Staggered Professional Development

Educational research indicates that one-shot professional development sessions do not bring change to classroom instruction, implementation, or student performance and learning (Ambule, 2017; Zarrow, 2014). Traditional means have historically been ineffective with their focus on awarding credit for showing up to workshops, conferences, or classes, as formal development opportunities have largely ignored whether teachers actually learned new skills, were able to apply them, and improved student outcomes (Horn & Arnett, 2017).

Research also indicates that many professional development activities for teachers do not incorporate available research on how to help teachers improve their teaching (Brown, 2016). By relying on generalized, off-the-shelf programs, traditional professional development does not target specific skills or expertise that an individual educator needs to improve their teaching practice (Horn & Arnett, 2017).

Many schools are moving away from traditional one-shot professional development and are focusing on staggered professional development, which consists of a series of focused workshops held by guest speakers or a school staff member on a regular interval to develop more comprehensive learning and a deeper sense of learning on the topic (Ambule, 2017). Keeping in mind that less is more, planning a larger number of shorter sessions that focus on specific learning goals will be more effective for teachers (Brown, 2016). Leaving a few weeks between sessions provides time for teachers to plan content, try out any strategies learned in the workshop, receive feedback from peers and students, and adjust the content based on the needs of students (Ambule, 2017).

Teachers as Resources

Teachers serve as the best resources for any school and with some assistance, many teachers can deliver practical and useful training sessions full of experience-based strategies that have been successfully tried and tested in a classroom (Ambule, 2017). Allowing teachers to demonstrate their talents and what they know best directly benefits the teachers by having their skills and expertise recognized. At the same time, these teachers help the school by having a person conduct professional development sessions who understands the training needs of the staff, is familiar with them, and is able to customize the content accordingly (Ambule, 2017).

Timing

Professional development sessions should allow a teacher to be present physically, mentally, and with complete focus (Darling-Hammond et al., 2017). When scheduling sessions, teachers' boundaries of professional and personal time should be respected and holidays, weekends, extended school days, and reporting/assessment cycle times should be avoided. For a successful outcome, it is best to have in-service professional development sessions on days throughout the school calendar so that teachers can focus without worrying about juggling between daily classroom management and personal commitments (Ambule, 2017).

On a daily basis, teachers share a multitude of strategies, tools, technology, and resources; however, for effective and engaging professional development to take place, teachers need to make an effort to attend training sessions, particularly when they are not mandatory (Ambule, 2017). School administrators should give teachers a choice in selecting their own field of interest and level of learning expertise (i.e., beginner, intermediate, or advanced) as well as allow multiple opportunities to practice over time (Ambule, 2017; Brown, 2016).

Content

Professional development should be kept simple in that each year, administrators should identify and focus on one or two instructional priorities that teachers should learn, refine, or improve and include content that students will learn (Zarrow, 2014; Brown, 2016). Priorities and expectations should be selected with teacher input and clearly communicated throughout all levels of the school (Zarrow, 2014; Vislocky, 2013). To be highly effective, professional development content should not only align with the school's vision and mission, it should enable teachers the ability to create classroom content and implement practical strategies in the classroom immediately, thus, leading to effective results for the school, teachers, and students (Ambule, 2017).

At times educators feel pushed into professional development sessions that may not be relevant or useful. Some even feel deprived of professional development opportunities in their areas of interest due to budget and time commitment issues (Ambule, 2017). To attempt a resolution to this issue, schools should allocate teachers' resources a fixed amount of funds and a time allowance for professional development days (Ambule, 2017).

Environment

Although the main focus of professional development sessions is on teaching and learning, workshop ambiance, particularly in face-to-face environments, is essential to the success of the training. A comfortable environment with hands-on activities will promote effective learning and retention. Regular breaks to refresh mind and body will not only help avoid monotony and information overload but provide opportunities for teachers to develop professional networks and engage in meaningful interactions (Ambule, 2017).

Reporting

Reflections on learning during and after professional development sessions is a valuable tool for reporting mechanisms. Sharing strategies about what was learned and the impact it will have on the enhancement of pedagogical practices can be a very rewarding and invaluable experience (Ambule, 2017).

CONSIDERATIONS WHEN PLANNING EFFECTIVE PROFESSIONAL DEVELOPMENT

Teachers have many different learning styles and encounter a variety of circumstances in the classroom; therefore, any professional development initiatives must recognize that teaching is inherently complex and nuanced and promote the empowerment of teachers (Zarrow, 2014). New initiatives must be carefully prioritized and ongoing support offered to make any professional development effective, lead to higher adoption rates by teachers and, ultimately, more integrated into classrooms (Vander Weide, 2017).

Transformative professional development can be implemented in any school or district and is created and implemented through purposeful engagement. It is differentiated across educator needs and transferable to every teacher's classroom to assist in helping students learn (Yaron, 2017).

Quality professional development happens with, not to, teachers (Yaron, 2017). Teacher leadership should be embraced, and teachers' professional expertise valued around the challenges and solutions that impact schools

(Hanover Research, 2012). An instructional leadership team with teacher voice can keep track of the realities in the classroom and build ownership in a professional development plan that aligns with school needs (Yaron, 2017). Allowing teachers to take part in the creation and sustainment of a plan that supports individuals will cultivate their desirability to teach and learn (Hannover Research, 2012).

Quality professional development links to a broader vision of where and how a school can grow over time. Planning professional development learning experiences as systemic processes will provide time to implement, rework, revise, and adapt practices that work for teachers (Yaron, 2017).

Before any professional development takes place, information should be collected about the audience that will be receiving the training (Vander Weide, 2017). Effective teachers want professional development opportunities that are applicable to their situation and classroom and that will help improve the quality of education they provide to their students (Meador, 2017b).

When administrators know what knowledge and skills it is that teachers need, planning and implementation is more effective, and teachers are more likely to want to attend and participate (Brown, 2016).

Sessions tailored to the technical capabilities and specific needs of teachers with activities and materials that are relevant to the classroom experience will create a more meaningful training (Vander Weide, 2017; Morrison, 2015). To strengthen training sessions, administrators should plan for more than one session of professional development as well as how to address the uneasiness some teachers may feel while adapting to a new way of teaching (Vander Weide, 2017).

During training, differentiated instruction should be used to account for the varying levels of technical abilities and understanding by teachers. Being prepared to adequately address the variety of skills and confidence levels of a diverse population has a significant impact on participant experience (Vander Weide, 2017).

Trainings should contain a wide array of opportunities for teachers to engage with one another in dynamic and respectful ways, including time to share thoughts with a partner and small group break outs where a step-by-step approach can be used to analyze potential solutions to a shared problem (Responsive Classroom, 2015). Using interactive learning compositions will create positive risk-taking environments, honest, respectful dialogue, and active engagement between the instructor, teachers, and the content (Responsive Classroom, 2015).

Teachers should be allowed time to employ the knowledge of what they learn in training. Sessions should be structured into multiple segments that first show how things should be done, then allow time for teachers to apply that skill. Segmented training is particularly effective when teachers are able to work on a project that can be taken from the training and immediately used in the classroom (Vander Weide, 2017).

Quality development opportunities create space and time for genuine collaboration that can lead to meaningful dialogue regarding best practices, strategies, assessments, curriculum design, and greater cohesiveness and collaboration between staff. Collaboration has the capacity to transform school culture through relationships and strategically working together to meet the needs of students (Yaron, 2017; Vislocky, 2013). When developing professional growth experiences, administrators must remember that implementation takes time and requires a collective growth mind-set (Dweck, 2006). Sharing challenges, celebrating successes, and making implementation visible are all an important part of the process (Yaron, 2017).

Educational staff development should be teacher led and use a variety of methods that will create engaging events in the classroom (Zarrow, 2014; Vislocky, 2013). Teaching takes place in the classroom and administrators seeking to provide professional development for their staff may consider sessions that use a classroom approach, as this method of delivery mimics what happens in the classroom, demonstrates methods of observation, reflection, and discussion as well as clarifies the school's mission and vision statement (Responsive Classroom, 2015; Darling-Hammond et al., 2017).

Research has shown that modeling by a colleague who has already mastered a particular method or skill plays a vital role in helping educators understand new instructional methods (Kaplan, 2017). By demonstrating new practices, teachers participate in active learning and are better able to understand how new practices can be implemented in real classrooms (Kaplan, 2017).

Through this model of professional development, teachers will be encouraged to interact and collaborate with other teachers and not isolate themselves within their own grades. Teachers will be inspired to learn new approaches or techniques from others that have varied backgrounds, experiences, and knowledge. By using local resources instead of outside consultants, teachers are more likely to engage in active participation, changing dialogue from the discussion of problems to brainstorming solutions (Morrison, 2015).

Workshops, coaching, classroom observations, and other developmental activities should take place in an ongoing continuum that includes instructional goals, instruction, and assessment with a continuous feedback loop that is sustained and adjusted over time to support changing needs and circumstances (Yaron, 2017). The creation of a feedback loop helps teachers monitor implementation and allows administrators to use teacher observations and student data to provide teachers with information on whether changes are having an effect on student achievement (Zarrow, 2014). The inclusion of a loop also provides insights into what teachers are struggling with, and gives administrators the opportunity to communicate that the knowledge gaps will be addressed (Vander Weide, 2017).

Providing opportunities to obtain feedback and further improve knowledge and skills creates a less overwhelming experience, presents the opportunity for hands-on learning, and enables knowledge to be delivered in smaller chunks (Vander Weide, 2017). This practice will promote a shift in school culture that effectively cultivates teacher skills, knowledge, and personalities in a way that manages a broader shared vision (Yaron, 2017).

Follow-up sessions after the initial training should also be conducted so teachers learn the information again and are able to collaborate with other teachers. Administrators may consider creating a Professional Learning Community (PLC), to ensure ongoing support to colleagues is offered and received (Vander Weide, 2017). PLCs will also provide teachers an opportunity to develop personal action plans, report back the result of implementing those plans, and reflect and receive feedback (support) from colleagues (Vislocky, 2013). A deliberate effort to support teacher implementation can also be made through the implementation of training events, coaching, principal observation, staff and grade-level meetings, and evaluation systems (Zarrow, 2014; Meador, 2017d).

Continued on-going professional development is necessary to provide teachers sufficient time to learn and implement new strategies (Zarrow, 2014; Vislocky, 2013; Meador, 2017b). Research has concluded that teachers may need as many as fifty hours of instruction, practice, and coaching before a new teaching strategy can be mastered and implemented in class (Zarrow, 2014).

Micro-Credentials

To help teachers learn and become proficient in relevant skills, there has been an emerging movement in exploring a competency-based, on-demand, personalized, and shareable professional learning system using micro-credentials (Schwartz, 2017). Professional development through micro-credentialing provides personalized development opportunities that match teachers' specific needs, allows teachers to drive their own development, shows areas of expertise, and advances their careers according to their skills (Horn & Arnett, 2017).

Micro-credentials provide an opportunity for teachers to engage in rigorous, self-paced, job-embedded professional learning that is related to the daily skills needed in the classroom (Schwartz, 2017). Through micro-credentials, teachers are able to earn recognition for skills that are acquired through formal and informal learning opportunities, to personalize professional learning, and take what they learned and apply it in the classroom (Acree, 2016).

Micro-credentials are rooted in classroom practice, and teachers will no longer have to attend workshops and receive credit for just being there. Instead, teachers must take learning back to the classroom, try it out, submit evidence, receive feedback from peers, and refine their approach (Schwartz, 2017).

Micro-credentials enable professional development providers to see the connections teachers make to their own practice by having teachers submit reflections and artifacts that demonstrate how they have integrated the learned practice into the classroom (Schwartz, 2017; Acree, 2016). A wide variety of artifacts may be submitted to demonstrate a teacher's knowledge and skill, such as poems, pictures, written personal reflections, and videotaped teaching (Acree, 2016). Teachers may be asked to resubmit their artifacts if the evidence of learning is not strong enough to demonstrate their experiences (Schwartz, 2017).

Through reflections, teachers are not being awarded for summarizing the content of the session, rather they are being encouraged to think critically and uncover exactly what was helpful and make applications to the practice of teaching (Acree, 2016). Although teachers may employ this process on their own, micro-credentials provide the opportunity for facilitated, structured reflections where teachers get meaningful feedback (Acree, 2016).

Effective Professional Development for Blended Learning

With the increase of blended learning in classrooms, professional development for effective implementation is critical (Mekhitarian, 2016). To help traditional teachers transition more effectively to blended teaching, administrators should consider incorporating training into professional development sessions. Effective blended-learning professional development should include learning experiences that focus on instructional approaches, challenge how teachers view instruction, and create opportunities to understand student perspectives on learning in a blended setting (Mekhitarian, 2016). Experiencing blended learning as learners can inform teachers' planning of rigorous, project-based learning opportunities and the necessary supports for student success (Mekhitarian, 2016).

Administrators can significantly impact a teacher's understanding of blended learning by modeling innovative best practices and creating opportunities for observations of disruptive classrooms. An important part of professional development in blended learning is providing the opportunity for teachers to observe peers at other school sites and have exposure to a wide range of approaches and philosophies used in blended learning (Mekhitarian, 2016).

Training on instructional practices should include a technology component for students and teachers to ensure smooth lesson transitions, minimal student frustration, and effective planning. Technological fluency is critical for success, and training sessions should be grounded in instructional practice with clear connections to how technology can augment and enlighten student learning opportunities (Mekhitarian, 2016).

BENEFITS OF EFFECTIVE PROFESSIONAL DEVELOPMENT

Providing educators with innovative tools and supporting them in skill development so that those tools can be used effectively in the classroom, has a direct and positive influence on student achievement (Darling-Hammond et al., 2017). Empowered and confident teachers can bring new ideas and innovations to their instruction as well as reach students they were once unable to with traditional teaching methods. Advanced technology and modern teaching tools help to create diverse and motivating lessons that engage students in novel approaches (Vander Weide, 2017).

Effective professional development should account for individualism and meet the teachers where they are and take them where they need to go. Effective professional development that is applicable to teachers' individual situations, resonates with them, and provides the resources to take what they have learned back to the classroom and apply it will improve teacher quality (Meador, 2017b). If schools and teachers establish a collaborative, intellectually stimulating environment for quality teachers, successful learning will take place (Zarrow, 2014). Teacher participation in effective professional development will lead to effective classroom practices, which will then lead to student success (Ambule, 2017).

FINAL THOUGHTS

Professional development must be an ongoing experience for educators, as short, one-time professional development experiences are less likely to impact instruction (Kaplan, 2017). Teachers must be given enough time to efficiently absorb and practice new methods and experience a continuous process filled with extended learning opportunities. With the mastery of new skills and instructional methods, teachers will be able to positively impact student learning and success.

Job-embedded professional development provides teachers with the opportunity to apply new instructional methods in their classes and helps bridge the gap between understanding a new method or concept and actually implementing it in the classroom (Kaplan, 2017). During this implementation stage, it is essential that administrators provide support to ensure that a new instructional method will be effective in the classroom.

Professional development content must be relevant and specific to a goal, discipline, grade level, or developmental stage and address the needs of educators and students (Darling-Hammond et al., 2017). Engrossing and varied approaches can be used to support learning and present content in a way that complements teachers' individual learning styles. Teachers' initial exposure to a concept should be engaging so that they may make sense of any new ideas or practices being taught (Kaplan, 2017). Collaboration is an excellent way to provide support for teachers, particularly those that are new to the profession. Sufficient time to have effective and meaningful conversations will lead to better teaching, problem resolution, and student learning and success.

With the emergence of micro-credentials, teachers have a new and innovative way to become proficient in relevant skills through personalized development opportunities that allow teachers to meet their needs on their own terms and advance their careers. Through informal and formal learning opportunities, teachers are able to apply what they learned in the classroom; become more effective teachers; and increase student learning and, ultimately, student success and teacher retention.

POINTS TO REMEMBER

- Professional development in education is essential for producing highly qualified teachers that must meet the state and federal teacher standards of competency established by the federal Department of Education.
- Quality professional development happens with, not to, teachers. Teachers' professional expertise and direct knowledge of classroom experiences and activities should be valued and embedded into training. Professional development opportunities must be applicable to classroom situations and improve the quality of education provided to the students.
- Quality professional development opportunities create genuine collaboration with meaningful dialogue regarding best practices, strategies, and curriculum design. Enhanced cohesiveness and collaboration between teachers has the capacity to transform school culture and meet the needs of students.
- Professional development through the use of micro-credentials provides personalized development opportunities, rigorous, self-paced, and job-embedded professional learning that is related to needed daily classroom skills.
- Effective blended-learning professional development includes learning experiences focused on instructional approaches and creates opportunities to understand student perspectives on learning in a blended setting. Experiencing blended learning as learners, teachers will engage in project-

based learning opportunities and receive the necessary supports for student success.

Chapter Twelve

Keeping Teachers on the Straight and Narrow

Understanding the Fundamentals of School Law

Every student has the right to a free, public education. More specifically, the rights of students with disabilities to receive the same educational opportunities as those students without disabilities has been recognized by Congress, which has stated that having a disability in no way diminishes the inherent right to participate or contribute to society (National Center for Learning Disabilities, 2006; American Psychological Association, 2017).

Improving educational results for individuals, particularly students with disabilities, is an essential element of national policy and ensures equality of opportunity, full participation, independent living, and economic self-sufficiency for individuals with disabilities (National Center for Learning Disabilities, 2006; American Psychological Association, 2017).

It is imperative that all educators and administrators know the special education laws, as they preserve the rights of students and their families and help integrate students with disabilities into society without segregation. Although laws are slightly different between states, the acts passed by Congress seek to standardize the treatment of students with disabilities across the country (Masters in Special Education, 2017).

THE ELEMENTARY AND SECONDARY EDUCATION ACT (ESEA)

In 1965, President Johnson's "War on Poverty" included the Elementary and Secondary Education Act of 1965 (ESEA), which also focused on providing equality of education, accountability, and high academic standards for students (Social Welfare History Project, 2016). ESEA was enacted to combat the achievement gap between low-income, neglected, and homeless families and white, higher-income families (Gamson, McDermott, & Reed, 2015; ASCD, 2017).

In addition to the enactment of ESEA, not only was federal funding for education established, several specific Titles were enacted. Title I focused on the skills and knowledge gap, Title II gave money to schools for libraries and textbooks and funded mandatory preschool, while Title III zeroed in on centers' and schools' ability to increase attendance (Social Welfare History Project, 2016). Title IV was responsible for funding research and training, Title V offered grant monies, while Title VI offered definitions and explanations of the entire act (Social Welfare History Project, 2016).

Every five years the act was evaluated and updated to reflect the changing language of the times, presidential foci, and population needs. In 1969, under President Nixon, funding for refugees and low-rent public housing was accepted with Title II, while Title VI acknowledged the importance of education for students with disabilities (Social Welfare History Project, 2016). The 1973 version of ESEA also included Section 504, which stated that any public education facility that accepted public monies was mandated to provide accommodations to students with disabilities to ensure access to education equal to that of non-disabled peers (U.S. Department of Education, 2016b).

Section 504

Section 504 of the 1973 version of ESEA protects the rights of individuals with disabilities in programs and activities that receive federal financial assistance from the U.S. Department of Education (U.S. Department of Education, 2010). Both private and public entities are prohibited from discriminating on the basis of disability (United Federation of Teachers, 2017). The statute provides that an otherwise qualified individual with a disability shall not be excluded from the participation in, be denied the benefits of, or be subjected to discrimination based on the fact that they have a disability (U.S. Department of Education, 2010).

Section 504 also requires recipients of federal funding to provide students with disability-appropriate educational services designed to meet their individual needs in the same way as students without disabilities (U.S. Department of Education, 2010). To fulfill this obligation, special education team members, along with a child's parent, create a 504 plan that provides services and changes to the student's learning environment (Understood, 2017).

Unlike Individual Education Plans (IEP), there is no standard 504 plan and the plans do not have to be a written document; however, similar to IEPs, 504 plans must be reviewed within a specific time frame and reevaluated when needed (Understood, 2017). A 504 plan must have specific accommodations and supports/services, and must designate the person who will perform those services, as well as a schedule for implementation (U.S. Department of Education, 2010).

Section 504 covers a broad population, but its protections are less specific than under the Individuals with Disabilities Act of 1990 (IDEA) (National Center for Learning Disabilities, 2006). Although the primary sources of students with disabilities rights fall under IDEA, students are also eligible for special education under Section 504. Conversely, students with disabilities are a small subsection of the population protected by the Americans with Disabilities Act, but the obligations imposed on public schools under Section 504 and the ADA are virtually identical (United Federation of Teachers, 2017).

EDUCATION FOR ALL HANDICAPPED CHILDREN ACT

Passed by Congress in 1975, this was the first special education law specifically for students with physical and mental disabilities (Masters in Special Education, 2017). The law stated that public schools must provide students with disabilities the same opportunities for education as other students and that schools that received federal funds must provide one free meal a day (Masters in Special Education, 2017).

The Education for All Handicapped Children Act of 1975 ensured that special education services were available to children with disabilities (U.S. Department of Education, 2007). Under this Act, public schools were required to provide fair, appropriate services, equal access to education, and the least restrictive school environment to students (U.S. Department of Education, 2007).

INDIVIDUALS WITH DISABILITIES EDUCATION ACT

The EHA was renamed as the Individuals with Disabilities Education Act (IDEA) in 1990 to improve upon special education and the services available for students with disabilities. Additional amendments were later passed in 1997 and again in 2004 to ensure equal access to education (Disabilities, Opportunities, Internetworking, and Technology, 2017; National Center for Learning Disabilities, 2006).

Under law, states and public agencies were mandated to provide early intervention, special education, and related services to more than 6.5 million eligible infants, toddlers, children, and youth with disabilities (National Center for Learning Disabilities, 2006). Under Part B of IDEA, all public schools receiving federal funding must supply a free appropriate public education to all students with disabilities, including those students with autism, specific learning disabilities, and speech and language impairment (United Federation of Teachers, 2017). Part B emphasizes that special education and related services are designed to meet students' unique needs and prepare them for further education, employment, and independent living (United Federation of Teachers, 2017).

IDEA also guaranteed a free education tailored to individual needs and delivered in the least restrictive environment with students being placed in a typical education setting with non-disabled students when feasible (National Center for Learning Disabilities, 2006; American Psychological Association, 2017; Master's in Special Education, 2017). The same high academic achievement standards, clear performance goals, and the opportunity to achieve them, must be consistent between students with disabilities and the standards and expectations set forth for all students in the educational system (National Center for Learning Disabilities, 2006; American Psychological Association, 2017).

IDEA mandates that each student that qualifies have an IEP that clearly defines in objective, measurable terms the learning outcomes that students with disabilities are expected to achieve as well as contain specific methods for tracking student progress (National Center for Learning Disabilities, 2006; Master's in Special Education, 2017). IDEA also mandates parent participation in developing a student's IEP and that student progress is reported to parents as frequently as it would be to the parents of those students without IEPs (National Center for Learning Disabilities, 2006; U.S. Department of Education, 2010).

1997 and 2004 Amendments to IDEA

Significant changes were made to IDEA in 1997, and again in 2004, concerning parentally placed private school students and local educational authorities (LEAs) who were now required to consult with private school officials prior to conducting activities to locate, identify, and evaluate students living in the state who may be suspected of having a disability (U.S. Department of Education, 2010).

School districts must provide parentally placed in-district private school students with disabilities a genuine opportunity for equitable participation in their special education programs (U.S. Department of Education, 2010). In addition, private school students with a disability must have a service plan that meets IEP content requirements and is developed, reviewed, and revised consistent with IEP process requirements (U.S. Department of Education, 2010). Support initiatives and transition plans and services for identifying appropriate employment and available community resources must now be included in a student's IEP (U.S. Department of Education, 2010; IDEA, n.d.).

NO CHILD LEFT BEHIND ACT OF 2001

The Elementary and Secondary Education Act, was updated and signed in 2001, and became known as the No Child Left Behind Act (2001) (Klein, 2015). This act now required school accountability for the academic performance of all students, including those students with disabilities (Masters in Special Education, 2017). Routine assessments were required in every state that tests third- through eighth-grade students in reading and math and again once during high school (Klein, 2015). Not only were incentives provided for schools to demonstrate progress in students with disabilities, students were now allowed to seek alternative options if schools were not meeting their academic, social, or emotional needs (Masters in Special Education, 2017).

The major focus of NCLB was to close student achievement gaps by providing all students with a fair, equal, and significant opportunity to obtain a high-quality education and achieve academic proficiency (Klein, 2015). Federal education funds may be used in ways schools deem appropriate to improve student achievement and success (Klein, 2015).

EVERY STUDENT SUCCEEDS ACT (ESSA)

In December 2015, NCLB was amended through Public Law 114-95, and became the Every Student Succeeds Act (ESSA) (U.S. Department of Education, 2015a; Gamson et al., 2015). ESSA reiterated the need to fully prepare all students for success and set forth the requirement that educators teach to all students the same academic content and maintain the same high academic standards to be successful in higher education and the workforce (Gamson et al., 2015; U.S. Department of Education, 2015a).

Those standards set by teachers must promote access to the general education curriculum and, for those students with disabilities, be designated in the individualized education program developed for each student (Gamson et al., 2015). Student proficiency goals must be clarified and based on the same definition of grade-level proficiency for all students (U.S. Department of Education, 2015a). Vital information is now guaranteed to be afforded to educators, families, and students through statewide assessments that measure students' progress toward those high standards.

Under ESSA, states have the opportunity to collaboratively establish reasonable goals and objectives in alignment with student needs (Klein, 2016). This autonomy assists teachers in designing personalized IEPs that will encourage students to be lifelong learners and IEP teams will be in a position to make critical decisions regarding students' academic assessment and social emotional needs (Alvarez, 2016).

ESSA (2015) has created the power to ensure that all students, regardless of race, family income, home language, or disability status, receive the equal education they need and deserve (Students Can't Wait, 2015; U.S. Department of Education, 2015a). States are held to a higher standard of accountability in that they must establish student performance goals, hold schools accountable for student achievement, and include comprehensive measures of student performance beyond test scores (ASCD, 2017).

Systems of accountability hold schools to higher achievement standards for all students and ensure progress for those students that are behind (Students Can't Wait, 2015). Accountability systems cannot raise student achievement or reduce inequities in learning opportunities but can hold schools accountable and set clear expectations that the achievement bar for all students must be raised (Students Can't Wait, 2015). Systems must be designed in a way that any disparities in education are apparent and a disservice to education is not created by hiding student achievement gaps (U.S. Department of Education, 2015a).

Under ESSA, there is one exception to the use of the same achievement standards for all students. Those students with the most significant cognitive disabilities, may be provided with alternative achievement standards that are in alignment with challenging academic content standards (Gamson et al., 2015; ASCD, 2017). Alternative standards must promote access to the general education curriculum and be set forth in the IEP for each student, ensuring that the student is on track to pursue postsecondary education or employment (Gamson et al., 2015; ASCD, 2017).

To enable the inclusion and participation of all students in assessments, appropriate accommodations must be provided. Using UDL is one way to ensure success for students with disabilities, as any barriers to instruction should be reduced and the high achievement expectations for all students will be maintained (Gamson et al., 2015; ASCD, 2017).

TITLE 1 OF THE ELEMENTARY AND SECONDARY EDUCATION ACT

Title I of the Elementary and Secondary Education Act of 1965 (ESEA), as amended by NCLB and then ESSA, is the largest educational program assisting disadvantaged children (Sonnenberg, 2016). Title I provides funding for the improved learning of students at risk of educational failure, including those in poverty-stricken schools, students with disabilities, and students and families in need of literacy services (Sonnenberg, 2016; U.S. Department of Education, 2015a).

Title I funds may be used to implement systems of support addressing the academic, social-emotional, behavioral, and mental health needs of all students; improve the quality and effectiveness of school community partnerships; and offer professional development for all relevant school personnel (U.S. Department of Education, 2015a; Lexia, 2016).

FERPA

The Family Educational Rights and Privacy Act of 1974 (FERPA) is a federal law that prohibits the improper disclosure of personally identifiable information contained in student records and applies to all educational agencies and institutions that receive federal funds (United Federation of Teachers, 2017; U.S. Department of Education, 2015b). FERPA gives parents certain rights over student educational records, unless there is a court order or state law that specifically provides otherwise. In general, private and parochial elementary and secondary schools do not receive federal funding and are thus not subject to FERPA (U.S. Department of Education, 2015b; Gjelten, 2017).

Under FERPA, parents have the right to inspect and review a student's educational records within 45 school days following the receipt of a request by the school (U.S. Department of Education, 2015b). Schools are required to provide parents with copies of educational records including the student's transcript, temporary school record, health records, tests, evaluations, discipline records and records pertaining to special education eligibility or programs (Massachusetts Department of Education, 2013).

Parents have the right to request that inaccurate or misleading information in the student's education records be amended but cannot challenge a grade, an individual's opinion, or a substantive decision made by a school about a student (U.S. Department of Education, 2015b). The improper disclosure of personally identifiable information from educational records is prohibited, and information that educators obtain through personal knowledge, observation, or hearsay, is not protected under FERPA (U.S. Department of Education, 2015b).

While FERPA generally requires consent of the parent before disclosing personally identifiable information, school officials, including teachers, administrators, staff members, and outsourced institutional services, are able to access personally identifiable information without prior written consent provided the school has a legitimate educational interest in the information (U.S. Department of Education, 2015b; United Federation of Teachers, 2017). School officials are deemed to have a legitimate educational interest if there is a need to review the record to fulfill a professional responsibility (U.S. Department of Education, 2015b). Schools are also permitted to disclose personally identifiable information without consent to another school in which the student seeks or intends to enroll (U.S. Department of Education, 2015b).

Schools may also disclose directory information, including a student's name, address telephone number and dates of attendance without consent; however, parents must be told what is considered directory information and provide parents with a reasonable amount of time to request the school not disclose that directory information (United Federation of Teachers, 2017).

COPYRIGHT LAW FOR TEACHERS

The Copyright Act of 1976, codified by the Constitution, provides authors, artists, inventors, and others who have created published or unpublished original works fixed in a tangible medium of expression certain exclusive rights and sets forth provisions for fair use (Wistrom, 2015). Original works of authorship including literary works (including computer software and compilations); music; dramatic works; pantomimes; choreographic work; pictorial, graphic, and sculpture works (such as maps and blueprints); motion pictures and other audio/visual works; sound recordings; and architecture (Wistrom, 2015). Works such as ideas or facts in the public domain, words, names, slogans or other short phrases, and government works cannot be copyrighted (Wistrom, 2015).

Although copyrights can be registered, there is no special or formal process to copyright an original piece of work, and copyright protection is conferred automatically at the moment of creation. It is no longer necessary for copyright symbols or phrases such as 'all rights reserved' to be included, and, unless it is explicitly clear that a piece of work is not copyrighted, teachers should always assume that any original, creative work is indeed copyrighted (Wistrom, 2015).

Copyrights do not last forever, and in 1998, the Sonny Bono Copyright Term Extension Act extended past copyright protection terms to the duration of the author's life plus seventy years (Wistrom, 2015). At the end of that time, or in the event the work did not initially meet copyright requirements, original works go into the public domain and become public property available for use by anyone (Wistrom, 2015). This is of particular importance to teachers, and specifically English teachers, as many of the literary works that students may be studying before the 20th century can be distributed and used in any manner the teacher feels necessary (Wistrom, 2015).

The Copyright Act provides five exclusive rights to the creators of a work including the right to reproduce; create derivative works; sell, lease, or rent copies of the work to the public; perform the work publicly; and display the work publicly (Wistrom, 2015). This means that administrators, teachers, and students cannot do anything that would violate these rights, although there is a special exception for the educational use of copyrighted materials called the fair use rule (Wistrom, 2015).

The fair use rule allows persons other than the copyright holder to make limited use of a copyrighted work without permission for teaching, research, scholarship, or criticism purposes as well as multiple classroom copies (Wistrom, 2015). The minimum standards of educational fair use state that single copies may be made for research or preparation for a class, and teachers may copy book chapters, magazine and newspaper articles, short stories and poems, diagrams, and pictures (Wistrom, 2015). Teachers may make multiple copies, one per student per course, for classroom use or discussion as long as poems are less than 250 words and two pages, prose is less than 2,500 words or an excerpt, and only one diagram/picture is copied from a single work (Wistrom, 2015).

Teachers are constantly faced with opportunities to uphold or violate copyright law, and school policy manuals typically state that teachers must uphold all copyright laws. Teachers could face serious legal consequences as well as termination of their job if they are found to be in violation of copyright law (Wistrom, 2015) It is important that teachers are aware of what constitutes fair use and abide by the rules set forth by their school system.

ETHICAL RESPONSIBILITIES OF TEACHERS

In addition to complying with legal requirements, teachers have a wide range of responsibilities to students that originate from a variety of federal, state, and local laws and regulations. Teachers are also obligated to observe ethical standards in codes of professional responsibility adopted by local school districts and state education departments (Gjelten, 2017).

There are also instances in which teachers learn things about students that might not be in their records and is therefore not protected under FERPA (Gjelten, 2017; U.S. Department of Education, 2015b). For instance, students may inadvertently reveal private information about their families, and ethical rules typically prohibit teachers from passing on any information about students learned through their work unless the disclosure is legally required (Gjelten, 2017). In the event that information reveals child maltreatment, abuse, or neglect, teachers and other school professionals are mandated to report what they have learned (Gjelten, 2017).

Teachers have a legal duty to supervise students in the same way that a sensible, careful parent would do under similar circumstances and ethical rules require teachers to show respect for all students, considering their age, gender, culture, and socioeconomic background. The duty to respect students also includes refraining from any kind of physical or verbal abuse, harassment, or illegal discrimination (Gjelten, 2017).

The Model Code of Ethics also specifies certain behaviors that teachers should avoid in order to prevent potential legal action and complications. Teachers should never touch a student without a clearly defined reason for doing, nor should they maintain personal relationships outside of school with students and their family members if those relationships will affect the teacher's objectivity or effectiveness (Gjelten, 2017). Under no circumstances, should a teacher ever engage in a romantic or sexual relationship with a student (Gjelten, 2017).

In order to ensure all students have a safe and productive learning environment, teachers have a responsibility to discipline any student who is disruptive to the classroom and endangers the safety of the other students. State laws and regulations do set limits on what teachers can do to carry out that discipline, and although most states outlaw spanking or other types of physical discipline, a significant majority of schools still allow it (Gjelten, 2017).

FINAL THOUGHTS

Every student has the right to a free, public education and students with disabilities should receive the same educational opportunities as those students without disabilities. Improving educational results for all individuals ensures equality of opportunity, full participation, independent living, and economic self-sufficiency for individuals with disabilities. As such, it is essential that all teachers know special education laws in order to preserve the rights of students.

A variety of laws, such as ESEA, Section 504, IDEA, and most recently ESSA, all protect the rights of individuals with disabilities in some way and prohibit educational entities from discriminating on the basis of disability. Through these laws, it is assured that appropriate educational services are designed to meet the individual needs of all students, with or without disabilities. IDEA also guarantees a free education tailored to individual needs and delivered in the least restrictive environment and that the same high academic achievement standards and clear performance goals must be consistent for all students in the educational system.

Teachers are constantly faced with opportunities to uphold or violate educational law. Failing to abide by federal and state law, including the copyright law and any ethical obligations derived from such laws, could cause teachers to be terminated from employment as well as face legal consequences.

POINTS TO REMEMBER

- ESEA (1965) provided federal funding for education, established a national curriculum, held schools accountable, increased equality, and extended provisions to students with disabilities.
- Section 504 asserts that an otherwise qualified individual with a disability shall not be excluded from participation in, be denied the benefits of, or be subjected to discrimination in education based on the fact that he or she has a disability.
- IDEA, Part B, mandates that all public schools receiving federal funding must supply a free appropriate public education to all students with disabilities, including those students with autism, specific learning disabilities, and speech and language impairment.
- ESSA restates the necessity of fully preparing all students for success and requires all students be taught the same academic content. Schools must also maintain the same high academic standards for all students regardless of race, family income, home language, or disability status.
- FERPA prohibits the improper disclosure of personally identifiable information contained in student records and applies to all educational agencies and institutions that receive federal funds. Parental consent is required to disclose personally identifiable information except when appropriate school personnel have a legitimate educational interest in the information and it is needed to fulfill a professional responsibility.
- Information that is not protected under FERPA and reveals child maltreatment, abuse, or neglect, must be reported, as educators and administrators are mandated reporters.
- The fair use exception to the Copyright Act allows educators to make limited use of a copyrighted work without permission for teaching, research, scholarship, or criticism purposes.

References

Abeysekera, L., and Dawson, P. (2014). Motivation and cognitive load in the flipped classroom: Definition, rationale, and a call for research. *Higher Education Research & Development , 34*(1). Retrieved from http://www.tandfonline.com/doi/abs/10.1080/07294360.2014.934336

Acree, L. (2016). *Seven lessons learned from implementing micro-credentials*. Raleigh, NC: Friday Institute for Educational Innovation at the NC State University College of Education. Retrieved from https://www.fi.ncsu.edu/wp-content/uploads/2016/02/microcredentials.pdf

Alber, R. (2015). 5 highly effective teaching practices. Retrieved from https://www.edutopia.org/blog/5-highly-effective-teaching-practices-rebecca-alber

Alber, R. (2016). Using graphic organizers correctly. Retrieved from https://www.edutopia.org/blog/using-graphic-organizers-correctly-rebecca-alber

Alber, R. (2017). 3 ways student data can inform your teaching. Retrieved from https://www.edutopia.org/blog/using-student-data-inform-teaching-rebecca-alber

Aliakbari, M., & Bozorgmanesh, B. (2015). Assertive classroom management strategies and students' performance: The case of an EFL classroom. *Cogent Education*. doi: 10.1080/2331186x.2015.1012899

Alrubail, R. (2015). Administrators, empower your teachers. Retrieved from https://www.edutopia.org/discussion/administrators-empower-your-teachers

Alvarez, B. (2016). Promising changes for special education under ESSA. *NeaToday*. Retrieved from http://neatoday.org/2016/06/30/special-education-essa

Ambule, M. (2017). Developing and delivering effective professional development for educators. Retrieved from https://www.edtechteam.com/blog/2017/11/developing-delivering-effective-professional-development-educators/

American Psychological Association. (2017). Individuals with disabilities education act (IDEA). Retrieved from http://www.apa.org/about/gr/issues/disability/idea.aspx

Aragon, S. (2016). *Teacher shortages: What we know*. Denver, CO: Education Commission of the States. Retrieved from https://www.ecs.org/wp-content/uploads/Teacher-Shortages-What-We-Know.pdf

Archer, A., & Hughes, C. (2011). *Explicit instruction: Effective and efficient teaching*. New York, NY: The Guilford Press.

ASCD. (2017). ESSA and accountability: Frequently asked questions. Retrieved from http://www.ascd.org/ASCD/pdf/siteASCD/policy/ESSA-Accountability-FAQ_May112016.pdf

Australian Capital Territory. (2016). *Great teaching by design: Evidence-based practices to improve student outcomes in Canberra's classrooms*. Canberra: Australian Capital Territory. Retrieved from http://www.det.act.gov.au/__data/assets/pdf_file/0006/854466/Great-Teaching-by-Design.pdf

References

Balasubramanian, K., Jaykumar, V., & Fukey, L. N. (2014). A study on "Student preference towards the use of Edmodo as a learning platform to create responsible learning environment." *Procedia: Social and Behavioral Sciences 144*(20), 416–422. Retrieved from https://doi.org/10.1016/j.sbspro.2014.07.311

Bhagi, U. (2016). 5 redefined roles of an educator in a blended classroom. Retrieved from https://elearningindustry.com/5-roles-educator-blended-classroom

Boyd-Dimock, V., & McGee, K. M. (2017). Leading change from the classroom: Teachers as leaders. Retrieved from http://www.sedl.org/change/issues/issues44.html

Brame, C. (2013). Flipping the classroom. *Vanderbilt University Center for Teaching*. Retrieved from https://cft.vanderbilt.edu/guides-sub-pages/flipping-the-classroom/

Bridgeland, J., Bruce, M., & Hariharan, A. (2013). *The missing piece: A national teacher survey on how social and emotional learning can empower children and transform schools.* Retrieved from https://www.casel.org/wp-content/uploads/2016/01/the-missing-piece.pdf

Brookhart, S. M. (2017). *How to give effective feedback to your students* (2nd ed.). Alexandria, VA: ASCD

Browder, D., Wood, L., Thompson, J., & Ribuffo, C. (2014). *Evidence-based practices for students with severe disabilities*. (Document No. IC-3). Gainesville: The University of Florida, Collaboration for Effective Educator, Development, Accountability, and Reform. Retrieved from http://ceedar.education.ufl.edu/wp-content/uploads/2014/09/IC-3_FINAL_03-03-15.pdf

Brown, R. (2016). Why does effective professional development in education matter? Retrieved from http://www.fastbridge.org/2016/07/why-does-effective-professional-development-in-education-matter/

Burns, M. (2015). The Common Core and digital skills development. Retrieved from https://www.edutopia.org/blog/common-core-digital-skills-development-monica-burns

Burton, T. (2015). *Exploring the impact of teacher collaboration on teacher learning and development*. (Doctoral dissertation). Retrieved from University of South Carolina: Columbia. h4p://scholarcommons.sc.edu/etd/3107

Byrne, R. (2014). Seven good student response systems that work on all devices. Retrieved from hhttp://www.freetech4teachers.com/2014/03/seven-good-student-response-systems.html#.WnelC6inFPY

CASEL (2018). SEL in action. Retrieved from https://casel.org/in-action/

CAST (2018). *Universal Design for Learning Guidelines version 2.2.* Retrieved from http://udlguidelines.cast.org

Camera, L. (2016). The teacher shortage crisis is here. *U.S. News*. Retrieved from https://www.usnews.com/news/articles/2016-09-14/the-teacher-shortage-crisis-is-here

Center for Comprehensive School Reform and Management. (2017). Role of principal leadership in improving student achievement. Retrieved from http://www.readingrockets.org/article/role-principal-leadership-improving-student-achievement

Center for Parent Information & Resources. (2017). ESSA: Every student succeeds act. Retrieved from http://www.parentcenterhub.org/essa-reauth/

Center for Teaching Quality, National Board for Professional Standards, and the National Education Association. (2014). *The teacher leadership competencies*. Retrieved from http://www.nbpts.org/wp-content/uploads/teacher_leadership_competencies_final.pdf

Conley, D. T. (2014). *A new era for educational assessment*. Retrieved from http://www.jff.org/sites/default/files/publications/materials/A-New-Era-for-Educational-Assessment-092414_0.pdf

Cook, B., Buysse, V., Klingner, J., Landrum, T., McWilliam, R., Tankersley, M., & Test, D. (2015). CEC's standards for classifying the evidence base practices in special education. *Remedial and Special Education, 36*(4), 220–234. doi: 10.177/0741932514557271

Cook, B., & Cook, S. (2013). Unraveling evidence-based practices in special education. *Journal of Special Education, 47*(2). 71–82. doi: 10.1177/0022466911420877

Cook, B., & Odom, S. (2013). Evidence-based practices and implementation science in special education. *Exceptional Children, 79*(2), 135–144. doi: 10.1177/001440291307900201

Council for Exceptional Children (2014). *Council for Exceptional Children standards for evidence-based practices in special education*. Arlington, VA: Council for Exceptional Children. Retrieved from https://www.cec.sped.org/~/media/Files/Standards/Evidence%20based%20Practices%20and%20Practice/EBP%20FINAL.pdf

Cox, S. (2017a). Earn parent support to help meet student needs. Retrieved from https://www.teacherready.org/parents-support/

Cox, S. (2017b). Why you should use "rounding" to build parent teacher relationships. Retrieved from https://www.teacherready.org/parent-teacher-relationships/

Cox, J. (2017c). What is the role of a teacher? Retrieved from https://www.thoughtco.com/what-is-the-role-of-a-teacher-2081511

Crowell, A. (2017). The hidden dangers of caring about your career too much. Retrieved from https://qz.com/958427/the-hidden-dangers-of-caring-about-your-career-too-much/

Curran, B. (2013, November 12). Teaching secrets: Start with the exit ticket. *Education Week*. Retrieved from https://www.edweek.org/tm/articles/2013/11/12/ctq_curran.html

Darling-Hammond, L., Hyler, M. E., & Gardner, M. (2017). *Effective teacher professional development*. Palo Alto, CA: Learning Policy Institute. Retrieved from https://learningpolicyinstitute.org/product/effective-teacher-professional-development-report

Deal, T. E., & Peterson, K. D. (2016). *Shaping school culture* (3rd ed.). San Francisco, CA: Jossey-Bass.

DeMatthews, D. (2014). Shared decision-making: What principals need to know. Retrieved from http://www.academia.edu/8506816/Shared_decision-making_what_principals_need_to_know_A_continuum_of_shared_decision-making

Diggs, C. (2015). How to overcome common challenges and engage parents. Retrieved from http://info.character.org/blog/topic/parent-involvement

Disabilities, Opportunities, Internetworking, and Technology. (2017). What is the individuals with disabilities act? Retrieved from http://www.washington.edu/doit/what-individuals-disabilities-education-act

Dodge, J. (2017). What are formative assessments and why should we use them? Tips for using formative assessments to help you differentiate instruction and improve student achievement. Retrieved from https://www.scholastic.com/teachers/articles/teaching-content/what-are-formative-assessments-and-why-should-we-use-them/

Dougherty, C. (2015). How school district leaders can support the use of data to improve teaching and learning. Retrieved from http://www.act.org/content/dam/act/unsecured/documents/Use-of-Data.pdf

Dunham, H. (2016). The importance of parent-teacher communication. Retrieved from https://au.mathletics.com/blog/importance-parent-teacher-communication

Durlak, J., Dymnicki, A., Taylor, R., Weissberg, R., & Schellinger, K. (2011). The impact of enhancing students' social and emotional learning: A meta-analysis of school based universal interventions. *Child Development, 82*, 405–432. Retrieved from https://www.researchgate.net/publication/49807966_The_Impact_of_Enhancing_Students%27_Social_and_Emotional_Learning_A_Meta-Analysis_of_School-Based_Universal_Interventions

Dweck, C. (2007). *Mindset: The new psychology of success*. New York, NY: Ballantine Books.

Dwyer, C., & William, D. (2017). Using classroom data to give systematic feedback to students to improve learning: The sooner the assessment the better for teacher and student. Retrieved from http://www.apa.org/education/k12/classroom-data.aspx

Dyer, K. (2014). 8 formative assessment data sources that help students become better learners. Retrieved from https://www.nwea.org/blog/2014/8-formative-assessment-data-sources-help-students-become-better-learners/

Dymnicki, A., Sambolt, M., & Kidron, Y. (2013). Improving college and career readiness by incorporating social and emotional learning. *College and Career Readiness and Success Center*. Retrieved from http://www.ccrscenter.org/products-resources/improving-college-and-career-readiness-incorporating-social-and-emotional

Education World. (2017). How to keep good teachers motivated. Retrieved from http://www.educationworld.com/a_admin/admin/admin289.shtml

Edwards, B., & Hinueber, J. (2015). Why teachers make good learning leaders. Retrieved from https://learningforward.org/docs/default-source/jsd-october-2015/why-teachers-make-good-learning-leaders.pdf

Emmer, E. T., & Sabornie, E. J. (Eds.). (2015). *Handbook of classroom management* (2nd ed.). New York: Routledge/Taylor & Francis.

Espelage, D., Rose, C., & Polanin, J. (2016). Social emotional learning program to promote prosocial and academic skills among middle school students with disabilities. *Remedial and Special Education, 37*(6), 323–332. doi: 10.1177/0741932515627475

Farrington, C., Roderick, M., Allensworth, E., Nagaoke, J. Keyes, T., Johnson, D., & Beechum, N. (2012). *Teaching adolescents to become learners: The role of noncognitive factors in shaping school performance: A critical literature review.* Chicago: The University of Chicago Consortium on Chicago School Research. Retrieved from https://consortium.uchicago.edu/sites/default/files/publications/Noncognitive%20Report.pdf

Francl, T. (2014). Is flipped learning appropriate? *Journal of Research in Innovative Teaching, 7*(1), 119–128.

Fuglei, M. (2014). How teachers use student data to improve instruction. Retrieved from https://education.cu-portland.edu/blog/classroom-resources/how-teachers-use-student-data-to-improve-instruction/

Gamson, D. A., McDermott, K. A., & Reed, D. S. (2015). The elementary and secondary education act at fifty: Aspirations, effects, and limitations, *RSF: The Russel Sage Foundation Journal of the Social Sciences, 1*(3): 1–29. doi: 10.7758/RSF.2015.1.3.01

Gardner-Webb University. (2017). How administrators can empower teachers. Retrieved from http://www.teachhub.com/working-together-administrators-role-empowering-teachers

Gaunt, R. (2017). What are the advantages and disadvantages of parent involvement in education. Retrieved from http://education.seattlepi.com/advantages-disadvantages-parent-involvement-education-4072.html

Geeraerts, K., Tynjala, P., Heikkinen, H., Markkanen, I., Pennanen, M., & Gijbels, D. (2015). Peer-group mentoring as a toll for teacher development. *European Journal of Teacher Education.* DOI:10.1080/19415257.2013.798741

Gjelten, EA. (2017). What are teachers' responsibilities to their student? Retrieved from https://www.lawyers.com/legal-info/education-law/school-law/teachers-have-many-responsibilities-to-their-students.html

Godbold, W. (2013, March 30). Empowered teachers will change the world. *SEEN.* Retrieved from http://www.seenmagazine.us/Articles/Article-Detail/articleid/2899/empowered-teachers-will-change-the-world

Gore, J., Llyod, A., Smith, M., Bowe, J., Ellis, H., & Lubans, D. (2017, November). Effects of professional development on the quality of teaching: Results from a randomized controlled trail of Quality Teaching Rounds. *Teaching and Teacher Education, 68*, 99–113. doi: 10.1016/j.tate.2017.08.007

Graham, S. Harris, K., and Chambers, A. (2016). Evidence-based practice and writing instruction. A review of reviews. In C. MacAuthur, S. Graham, & J. Fitzgerald (Eds.), *Handbook of writing research.* (211–226). New York, NY. The Guilford Press Publications, Inc.

Great Schools Partnership. (2014). Demonstration of learning. Retrieved from http://edglossary.org/demonstration-of-learning/

Green, T. R., & Allen, M. (2015). Professional development urban schools: What do teachers say? Retrieved from https://files.eric.ed.gov/fulltext/EJ1133585.pdf

Hanover Research. (2015). *Best practices in instructional coaching.* Arlington, VA: Hanover Research. Retrieved from https://www.educateiowa.gov/sites/files/ed/documents/Best%20Practices%20in%20Instructional%20Coaching%20-%20Iowa%20Area%20Education%20Agencies.pdf

Hanover Research. (2012). *Best practices in teacher leadership training and principal development.* Arlington, VA: Hanover Research. Retrieved from http://www.shaker.org/Downloads/BestPracticesTeacherLeadershipTrainingPrincipalDevelopment.pdf

Hare, J. (2017). Creating key partnerships with parents. Retrieved from http://teaching.monster.com/benefits/articles/6121

Harn, B., Parisi, D., & Stoolmiller, M. (2013). Balancing fidelity with flexibility and fit: What do we really know about fidelity of implementation in schools? *Exceptional Children, 79*(2), 181–193. doi: 10.177/001440291307900204

Hattie, J. (2015, October 28). We aren't using assessments correctly: There's a distinction between formative and summative assessments. *Education Week*. Retrieved from https://www.edweek.org/ew/articles/2015/10/28/we-arent-using-assessments-correctly.html

Hocket, J., & Doubet, K. (2017). 6 strategies for promoting student autonomy. Retrieved from https://www.edutopia.org/article/6-strategies-promoting-student-autonomy

Horn, M. B., & Arnett, T. (2017). Competency-based learning for teachers. Retrieved from http://educationnext.org/competency-based-learning-teachers-micro-credentials-professional-development/

Horn, M. B., & Staker, H. (2015). *Blended: Using disruptive innovation to improve schools*. San Francisco, CA: Jossey-Bass.

Horvath, V. S., & Caulfield, R. A. (2016). *Preparing teachers in today's challenging context: Key issues, policy directions, and implications for leaders of AASCU Universities*. Washington, DC: AASCU. Retrieved from https://www.aascu.org/AcademicAffairs/TeacherEdReport.pdf

Hozien, W. (2017). Student diversity in public schools. Retrieved from http://www.educationviews.org/student-diversity-public-schools/

Huseman, J. (2015). *How compatible are Common Core and technology?* Retrieved from http://hechingerreport.org/how-compatible-are-common-core-and-technology/

Hwang, G., Lai, C., and Wang, S. (2015). Seamless flipped learning: A mobile technology-enhanced flipped classroom with effective learning strategies. *Journal of Computer Education 2*(4), 449–473. doi: 1007/s40692-015-0043-0

IDEA: Individuals with Disabilities Act. (n.d.) *About IDEA*. Retrieved from http://sites.ed.gov/idea/about-idea/#IDEA-Purpose

Inclusive Schools Network. (2015). The principals' responsibilities in supporting quality instruction. Retrieved from http://inclusiveschools.org/the-principals-responsibilities-in-supporting-quality-instruction/

Jones, S. M., & Bouffard, S. M. (2012). Social and emotional learning in schools: From programs to strategies. *Social Policy Report, 26* (4). Retrieved from https://casel.org/social-and-emotional-learning-in-schools-from-programs-to-strategies/

Kaplan. (2017). The principles of effective professional development. Retrieved from https://www.kaplanco.com/ii/principles-of-effective-professional-development

Klein, A. (2015). No child left behind: An overview. *Education Week*. Retrieved from https://www.edweek.org/ew/section/multimedia/no-child-left-behind-overview-definition-summary.html

Klein, A. (2016). The every student succeeds act: An overview. *Education Week*. Retrieved from https://www.edweek.org/ew/issues/every-student-succeeds-act/index.html

Kumon. (2015). The importance of self-learning. Retrieved from https://www.kumon.com/resources/the-importance-of-self-learning/

Lambert, K. (2018). Why our teachers are leaving. Retrieved from http://www.educationworld.com/why-our-teachers-are-leaving

Larmer, J., Mergendoller, J. Boss, S. (2015). *Setting the standard for project based learning: A proven approach to rigorous classroom instruction*. Alexandria, VA: ASCD.

Lasry, N., Dugdale, M., & Charles, E. (2014). Just in time to flip your classroom. *The Physics Teacher, 52*(1), 34–37. Retrieved from https://arxiv.org/pdf/1309.0852

Learning Forward. (2017). Standards for professional learning. Retrieved from https://learningforward.org/standards

Lemov, D. (2015). *Teach like a champion 2.0: 62 techniques that put students on the path to college*. San Francisco, CA: Jossey-Bass

Levin, B. B., & Schrum, L. R. (2017). *Every teacher a leader: Developing the needed dispositions, knowledge, and skills for teacher leadership*. Thousand Oaks, CA: Corwin.

Lexia. (2016). Understanding the unique needs of Title I students. Retrieved from https://www.lexialearning.com/blog/understanding-unique-needs-title-i-students#

Lin, Y. J. (2014). Teacher involvement in school decision making. *Journal of Studies in Education, 4*(3). doi:10.5296/jse.v4i3.6179

Logan, L. (2017). 5 ways to use data to improve your teaching. Retrieved from https://www.amplify.com/viewpoints/5-ways-to-use-data-to-improve-your-teaching

Mackey, K. H. (2016). The relationships among instructional leadership, school culture, and student achievement in Kentucky elementary schools. Retrieved from https://digitalcommons.wku.edu/cgi/viewcontent.cgi?referer=https://www.google.com/&httpsredir=1&article=1111&context=diss

Magsamen, S. (2016, October). The parent-teacher relationship: Why it's more important than ever. *Working Mother*. Retreived from www.workingmother.com/parent-teacher-relationship-why-its-more-important-than-ever

Maheady, L., Rafferty, L., Patti, A., & Budin, S. (2016). Leveraging change: Influencing the implemtation of evidence-based practice to improve outcomes for students with disabilities. *Learning Dsiabilities: A Contemporary Journal, 14*(2), 109–120. Retrieved from http://www.ldw-ldcj.org/index.php/open-access-articles/8-testblog/61-leveraging-evidence-based-practices-from-policy-to-action.html

Martin, J., and Torres, A. (2015). What is student engagement and why is it important? Users guide and toolkit for the surveys of student engagement: The high school survey of student engagement (HSSSE) and the middle grades survey of student engagement (MGSSE). *National Association of Independent Schools*. Retrieved from https://www.nais.org/Articles/Documents/Member/2016%20HSSSE-report-full-FINAL.pdf

Martin, N., Schafer, N., McClowry, S., Emmer, E., Brekelmans, M., Mainhard, T., & Wubbels, T. (2016). Expanding the definition of classroom management: Recurring themes and new conceptualizations. *Journal of Classroom Interactions, 51*(1), 31–41. Retrieved from http://insightsintervention.com/insightsintervention.com/2%20Martin%20Definition%20of%20Classroom%20Management%20%202.pdf

Marzano Center. (2015). Student engagement: 5 ways to get and keep your students' attention. Retrieved from http://www.marzanocenter.com/2015/08/19/5-ways-to-get-and-keep-your-students-attention/

Marzano, R. J., Frontier, T., & Livingston, D. (2011). *Effective supervision: Supporting the art and science of teaching*. Alexandria, VA: ASCD.

Marzano, R., & Pickering, D. (2010). *The highly engaged classroom*. Bloomington, IN: Marzano Research Laboratory

Massachusetts Department of Education. (2013). Parent's notice of procedural safeguards. Retrieved from http://www.doe.mass.edu/sped/prb/pnps.pdf

Massachusetts Department of Education. (2017). Educator evaluation. Retrieved from http://www.doe.mass.edu/edeval/

Masters in Special Education. (2017). 5 important special education laws. Retrieved from https://www.masters-in-special-education.com/lists/5-important-special-education-laws/

McKnight, K., O'Malley, K., Ruzic, R; Horsely, M. K., Franey, J. J., & Bassett, K. (2016). Teaching in a digital age: How educators use technology to improve student learning. *Journal of Research on Technology in Education, 48*(3). doi: 10.1080/1531523.2016.1175856

Meador, D. (2017a). Cultivating highly successful parent teacher communication. Retrieved from https://www.thoughtco.com/tips-for-highly-successful-parent-teacher-communication-3194676

Meador, D. (2017b). How effective professional development improves teacher quality. Retrieved from https://www.thoughtco.com/professional-development-improves-teacher-quality-3194385

Meador, D. (2017c). How school leaders can help improve teacher quality. Retrieved from https://www.thoughtco.com/improving-teacher-quality-3194527

Meador, D. (2017d) Seven strategies to provide help for teachers. Retrieved from https://www.thoughtco.com/strategies-to-provide-help-for-teachers-3194529

Meador, D. (2017e). Suggestions for principals to provide teacher support. Retrieved from https://www.thoughtco.com/suggestions-for-principals-to-provide-teacher-support-3194528

Meador, D. (2017f). Pros and cons of teaching. Retrieved from https://www.thoughtco.com/pros-and-cons-of-teaching-3194702

Meadows Center for Preventing Educational Risk & George W. Bush Institute. (2016). *Middle school matter field guide: Research-based principles, practices and tools* (2nd ed.). Austin,

TX: Authors. Retrieved from http://www.meadowscenter.org/files/resources/1_FieldGuide.pdf

Meier, K. S. (2017). What are the duties of a teacher in classroom management? Retrieved from http://education.seattlepi.com/duties-teacher-classroom-management-4012.html

Meier, K. S. (2018, March 15). What is the role of teachers in education? *Houston Chronicle*. Retrieved http://work.chron.com/role-teachers-education-8807.html

Mekhitarian, S. (2016). 4 tips for developing effective professional development for blended learning. Retrieved from https://www.christenseninstitute.org/blog/4-tips-for-developing-effective-professional-development-for-blended-learning/

Meyer, A., Rose, D., & Gordon, D. (2014). *Universal design for learning: Theory and practice*. Wakefield, MA: CAST Professional Publishing.

Ministry of Education and British Columbia School Superintendent's Association (2015). Why classroom management is important. Retrieved from http://education.gov.gy/web/index.php/teachers/tips-for-teaching/item/1651-why-classroom-management-is-important

Morrison, C. D. (2014). From "sage on the stage" to "guide on the side": A good start. Retrieved from https://digitalcommons.georgiasouthern.edu/cgi/viewcontent.cgi?article=1011&context=ij-sotl

Morrison, N. (2015, June 10). The eight components of great professional development. *Forbes*. Retrieved from https://www.forbes.com/sites/nickmorrison/2015/06/10/the-eight-components-of-great-professional-development/2/#6dacd81f77b4

Nagro, S., Hooks, S., Fraser, D., & Cornelius, K. (2016). Whole-group response strategies to promote student engagement in inclusive classrooms. *Teaching Exceptional Children, 48*(5), 243–249. doi: 10.1177/0040059916640749

National Association of Elementary School Principals. (2011). *Student assessment: Using student achievement data to support instructional decision making*. Alexandria, VA: NAESP. Retrieved from http://www.naesp.org/sites/default/files/Student%20Achievement_blue.pdf

National Association of Secondary School Principals & National Association of Elementary School Principals. (2013). *Leadership matters: What the research says about the importance of principal leadership*. Alexandria, VA: Authors. Retrieved from http://www.naesp.org/sites/default/files/LeadershipMatters.pdf

National Center for Learning Disabilities. (2006). *IDEA Parent Guide: A comprehensive guide to your rights and responsibilities under the Individuals with Disabilities Act (IDEA 2004)*. New York: NCLD. Retrieved from https://www.ncld.org/wp-content/uploads/2014/11/IDEA-Parent-Guide1.pdf

National Center on Universal Design for Learning. (2017). UDL guidelines: Theory and practice. Retrieved from http://www.udlcenter.org/aboutudl/udlguidelines_theorypractice

National Conference of State Legislators. (2013). Preparing and licensing effective teachers. Retrieved from http://www.ncsl.org/research/education/preparing-and-licensing-effective-teachers.aspx

National Council for Accreditation of Teacher Education. (2014). Research supporting the effectiveness of teacher preparation. Retrieved from http://ncate.org/Public/ResearchReports/TeacherPreparationResearch/EffectivenessofTeacherPreparation/tabid/362/Default.aspx

Ness, M. (2018). *Think big with think alouds: A three step planning process that develops strategic reading*. Thousand Oaks, CA: Corwin.

Nicol, D. J., & Macfarlane-Dick, D. (2006). Formative assessment and self-regulated learning: a model and seven principles of good feedback practice. *Studies in Higher Education, 31*(2), 199-218. DOI: 10.1080/03075070600572090

Obiakor, F., Harris, M., Mutua, K., Rotatori, A., &Algozzine, B. (2012). Making inclusion work in general education classrooms. *Education and Treatment of Children , 35*, 477–490. Retrieved from https://www.thefreelibrary.com/Making+inclusion+work+in+general+education+classrooms.-a0301649979

O'Brien, A. (2014). When teachers and administrators collaborate. Retrieved from https://www.edutopia.org/blog/when-teachers-and-administrators-collaborate-anne-obrien

Ohio Department of Education. (2016). Sample best practices for parent involvement in school. Retrieved from https://education.ohio.gov/Topics/Other-Resources/Family-and-

Community-Engagement/Getting-Parents-Involved/Sample-Best-Practices-for-Parent-Involvement-in-Sc

Pellegrino, J., & Hilton, M. (Eds.) (2013). *Education for life and work: Developing transferable knowledge and skills in the 21st century*. Washington, DC: National Academies Press. Retrieved from https://www.nap.edu/catalog/13398/education-for-life-and-work-developing-transferable-knowledge-and-skills

Phillips, M. (2014). My favorite kind of meeting: Individual conferences in action. Retrieved from https://www.literacyworldwide.org/blog/literacy-daily/2014/04/15/my-favorite-kind-of-meeting-individual-conferences-in-action

Pickens, I. (2015, September). The brief wondrous life of teachers' mental health: Supporting teachers experiencing emotional burnout. *Psychology Today*. Retrieved from https://www.psychologytoday.com/blog/revolutionary-thoughts/201509/the-brief-wondrous-life-teachers-mental-health

Pride Surveys. (2016a). 4 benefits of positive student-teacher relationships. Retrieved from https://www.pridesurveys.com/index.php/blog/4-beneficial-effects-of-student-teacher-relationships/

Pride Surveys. (2016b). Tips for strong parent-teacher cooperation and communication. Retrieved from https://www.pridesurveys.com/index.php/blog/parent-teacher-cooperation-communication/

ProSolutions Training. (2015). The benefits of building strong relationships with parents. Retrieved from www.prosolutionstraining.com/blog/2015/02/the-benefits-of-building-strong-relationships-with-parents.cfm

RTI Action Network. (2018). School transformation model. Retrieved from http://www.rtinetwork.org/about-us/school-transformation

Responsive Classroom. (2015). Lively learning for professional development. Retrieved from https://www.responsiveclassroom.org/lively-learning-for-professional-development/

Responsive Classroom. (2018). Principles and practices. Retrieved from https://www.responsiveclassroom.org/about/principles-practices/

Richert, K. (2017). How to create partnerships with parents and families. Retrieved from http://teaching.monster.com/counselors/articles/8144-how-to-create-partnerships-with-parents-and-families

Rizvi, M. (2016). Teacher leadership as professional development. Retrieved from hhttps://www.edutopia.org/blog/teacher-leadership-as-professional-development-marium-rizvi

Roscorla, T. (2017). 5 ways education leaders can support teachers. Retrieved from http://www.centerdigitaled.com/k-12/5-Ways-Education-Leaders-Can-Support-Teachers.html

Rosenshine, B. (2012). Principles of instruction: Research-based strategies that all teachers should know. *American Educator*. Retrieved from https://www.aft.org/sites/default/files/periodicals/Rosenshine.pdf

Samuels, C. A. (2016, February 24). ESSA spotlights strategy to reach diverse learners. *Education Week*. Retrieved from https://www.edweek.org/ew/articles/2016/02/24/essa-spotlights-strategy-to-reach-diverse-learners.html

Sarnovsky, D. (2016). What's happening in character: The essentials of building relationships with parents. Retrieved from http://info.character.org/blog/the-essentials-of-building-relationships-with-parents

Schaaf, R. (2018). Snapshots of understanding? 10 smart tools for digital exit slips. Retrieved from https://www.teachthought.com/technology/smart-tools-for-digital-exit-slips/

Scheeler, M., Budin, S., & Markelz, A. (2016). The role of teacher preparation in evidence-based practices in schools. *Learning Disabilities: A Contemporary Journal, 14* (2), 171–187. Retrieved from http://www.ldw-ldcj.org/index.php/open-access-articles/8-testblog/64-the-role-of-teacher-preparation-in-promoting-evidence-based-practice-in-schools.html

School Courses & Career Development. (2017). Roles and responsibilities for teachers in the classroom. Retrieved from http://www.sccdtraining.co.uk/roles-and-responsibilities-for-teachers/

References

Schwartz, K. (2016). 7 qualities that promote teacher leadership in schools. Retrieved from https://ww2.kqed.org/mindshift/2016/03/16/7-qualities-that-promote-teacher-leadership-in-schools/

Schwartz, K. (2017). Can micro-credentials create more meaningful professional development for teachers? Retrieved from https://ww2.kqed.org/mindshift/2017/02/15/can-micro-credentials-create-meaningful-professional-development-for-teachers/

Scott, E. (2013). Teachers on screen: Video could be key tool. Retrieved from http://hechingerreport.org/teachers-on-screen-video-could-be-key-tool/

Scruggs, T., Mastropieri, M., & Marshak, L. (2012). Peer-mediated instruction in inclusive secondary social studies learning: Direct and indirect learning effects. *Learning Disabilities Research & Practice, 27*, 12–20. doi: 10.1111/j.1540-5826.2011.00346.x

SimplyCircle. (2015). 5 benefits of regular communication with parents in your classroom. Retrieved from https://www.simplycircle.com/benefits-regular-communication/

Social Welfare History Project. (2016). Elementary and Secondary Education Act of 1965. Retrieved from http://socialwelfare.library.vcu.edu/programs/education/elementary-and-secondary-education-act-of-1965/

Sonnenberg, W. (2016). *Allocating grants for Title I*. Washington, DC: National Center for Education Statistics. Retrieved from https://nces.ed.gov/surveys/AnnualReports/pdf/titleI20160111.pdf

Sornson, B. (2015). The effects of using the essential skills inventory on teacher perception of high-quality classroom instruction. *Preventing School Failure, 59*(3), 161–167. doi:10.1080/1045988X.2014.886551

Starr, L. (2017). Activities to promote parent involvement. Retrieved from http://www.educationworld.com/a_curr/curr200.shtml

Stephens, T. (2015). Encouraging positive student engagement and motivation: Tips for Teachers. *Pearson 30 Review*. Retrieved from https://www.pearsoned.com/encouraging-positive-student-engagement-and-motivation-tips-for-teachers/

Stronge, J. H., Grant, L. W., & Xu, X. (2015a). The changing roles of teachers: What research indicates. Part I of II. *P21, 2*(13), 3. Retrieved from http://www.p21.org/news-events/p21blog/1791-the-changing-roles-of-teachers-what-research-indicates-part-i-of-ii

Stronge, J. H., Grant, L. W. & Xu, X. (2015b). The changing roles of teachers: What research indicates. Part II of II. *P21, 2*(13), 4. Retrieved from http://www.p21.org/news-events/p21blog/1792-the-changing-roles-of-teachers-what-research-indicates-part-ii-of-ii

Students Can't Wait. (2015). An introduction to school accountability under ESSA. Retrieved from https://studentscantwait.org/resource/introduction-school-accountability-essa/

Studer Group. (2018). AIDET communication. Retrieved from https://www.studergroup.com/aidet

Tek, B., (2014). An investigation of the relationship between school leadership, teacher job satisfaction, and student achievement. *Open Access Dissertations. Paper 221*. Retrieved from http://digitalcommons.uri.edu/cgi/viewcontent.cgi?article=1239&context=oa_diss

Thompson, J. G. (2017). Discipline tip: Involve parents. Retrieved from http://teaching.monster.com/benefits/articles/1899

Tomlinson, C. (2014). *The differentiated classroom: Responding to the needs of all learners* (2nd ed.). Alexandria, VA: ASCD.

Tucker, C. R. (2013). The basics of blended learning. *Educational Leadership, 70*(6) 57–60. Retrieved from http://www.ascd.org/publications/educational-leadership/mar13/vol70/num06/The-Basics-of-Blended-Instruction.aspx

Understood. (2017). What to expect at a due process hearing. Retrieved from https://www.understood.org/en/school-learning/your-childs-rights/dispute-resolution/what-to-expect-at-a-due-process-hearing

United Federation of Teachers. (2017). Federal laws, regulations, and policy guidance. Retrieved from http://www.uft.org/teaching/federal-laws-regulations-and-policy-guidance

U.S. Bureau of Labor Statistics. (2016a). High school teachers. Retrieved from https://www.bls.gov/ooh/education-training-and-library/high-school-teachers.htm

U.S. Bureau of Labor Statistics. (2016b). Kindergarten and elementary teachers. Retrieved from https://www.bls.gov/ooh/education-training-and-library/kindergarten-and-elementary-school-teachers.htm

U.S. Department of Education. (2007). *Twenty-five years of progress in educating children with disabilities through IDEA*. Retrieved from https://www2.ed.gov/policy/speced/leg/idea/history.html

U.S. Department of Education. (2010). *Thirty-five years of progress in educating children with disabilities through IDEA*. Retrieved from http://www2.ed.gov/about/offices/list/osers/idea35/history/idea-35-history.pdf

U.S. Department of Education. (2015a). Every Student Succeeds Act. Retrieved from https://www.ed.gov/essa?src=ft

U.S. Department of Education. (2015b). FERPA General Guidance for Parents. Retrieved from https://www2.ed.gov/policy/gen/guid/fpco/ferpa/parents.html

U.S. Department of Education. (2016a). Improving teacher preparation: Building on innovation. Retrieved from https://www.ed.gov/teacherprep

U.S. Department of Education. (2016b). *Parent and educator resource guide to section 504 in public elementary and secondary schools*. Retrieved from https://www2.ed.gov/about/offices/list/ocr/docs/504-resource-guide-201612.pdf

U.S. Department of Education (2017). *Reimaging the role of technology in education: 2017 national education technology plan update*. Retrieved from https://tech.ed.gov/files/2017/01/NETP17.pdf

U.S. Department of Education, Institute of Education Sciences, & National Center for Education Evaluation and Regional Assistance. (2003). Identifying and implementing educational practices supported by rigorous evidence: A user-friendly guide. *Coalition for Evidence-Based Policy*. Retrieved from https://www2.ed.gov/rschstat/research/pubs/rigorousevid/rigorousevid.pdf

Vander Weide, L. (2017). How to get started: Meaningful professional development for educators. Retrieved from https://www.chalk.com/resources/meaningful-professional-development-educators/

Venables, D. R. (2017). 8 of the most common sources of formative assessment data. Retrieved from https://www.teachthought.com/learning/8-frequent-sources-formative-assessment-data/

Vilorio, D. (2016). Teaching for a living. *U.S. Department of Labor: Bureau of Labor Statistics*. Retrieved from http://www.bls.gov/careeroutlook/2016/article/education-jobs-teaching-for-a-living.htm

Vislocky, E. (2013). Five key elements to successful embedded teacher professional development. Retrieved from: https://www.nwea.org/blog/2013/five-key-elements-to-successful-embedded-teacher-professional-development/

Watanabe-Crockett, L. (2017). 12 strong strategies for effectively teaching critical thinking skills. Retrieved from https://globaldigitalcitizen.org/12-strategies-teaching-critical-thinking-skills

Watkins, A. (2016). Role of the principal in beginning teacher induction. Retrieved from https://newteachercenter.org/wp-content/uploads/Role-of-Principal-in-Teacher-Induction.pdf

Watson, C. (2014). Effective professional learning communities? The possibilities for teachers as agents of change in schools. *British Educational Research Journal, 40*(1), 18–29. doi: 10.1002/berj.3025

Welborn, B. (2012, March 13). Six keys to successful collaboration. *Education Week*. Retrieved from https://www.edweek.org/tm/articles/2012/03/13/tln_collaboration.html

Weller, C. (2017, May). Teachers reveal how education has changed dramatically over the past 20 years. *Business Insider*. Retrieved from http://www.businessinsider.com/teachers-how-education-has-changed-2017-5

Wells, A. S., Fox, L., & Cordova-Cobo, D. (2016). How racially diverse schools and classrooms can benefit all students. Retrieved from https://tcf.org/content/report/how-racially-diverse-schools-and-classrooms-can-benefit-all-students/

Westervelt, E. (2016). Frustration. Burnout. Attrition. It's time to address the national teacher shortage. *New England Public Radio*. Retrieved from https://www.npr.org/sections/ed/2016/

09/15/493808213/frustration-burnout-attrition-its-time-to-address-the-national-teacher-shortage

What Works Clearing House (2015). *Procedures and standards handbook (Version 3.0)*. Retrieved from https://ies.ed.gov/ncee/wwc/Docs/ReferenceResources/wwc_scd_key_criteria_011017.pdf

What Works Clearing House (2017). *Procedures and standards handbook (Version 4.0)*. Retrieved from https://ies.ed.gov/ncee/wwc/Docs/ReferenceResources/wwc_procedures_handbook_v4_draft.pdf

Williams, K. (2017). 9 techniques for building solid parent-teacher relationships. Retrieved form https://www.scholastic.com/teachers/articles/teaching-content/9-techniques-building-solid-parent-teacher-relationships/

Wistrom, E. (2015). Copyright laws for teachers: What you need to know. Retrieved from http://www.brighthubeducation.com/teaching-methods-tips/6623-understanding-copyright-law-and-fair-use-for-teachers/

Wright, A. (2016). How principals can support teacher leaders: Lessons from Glenn O. Swing Elementary School. Retrieved from https://www.teachingquality.org/content/blogs/barnett-berry/how-principals-can-support-eacher-leaders-lessons-glenn-o-swing

Yaron, L. (2017, May 9). The 5 W's of quality of professional development. *Education Week*. Retrieved from https://www.edweek.org/tm/articles/2017/05/09/the-five-ws-of-quality-professional-development.html

Yoder, N. (2014). *Teaching the whole child: Instructional practices that support social-emotional learning in three teacher evaluation frameworks*. Washington, DC: Center on Great Teachers and Leaders Retrieved from https://gtlcenter.org/sites/default/files/TeachingtheWholeChild.pdf

Young, N. D., Michael, C. N., & Citro, T. A. (2018). *Emotions and education: Promoting positive mental health in students with learning disabilities*. Wilmington, DE: Vernon Press.

Zarrow, J. (2014). 5 strategies for better teacher professional development. Retrieved from https://www.teachthought.com/pedagogy/5-strategies-better-teacher-professional-development/

About the Authors

Nicholas D. Young, PhD, EdD, has worked in diverse educational roles for more than 30 years, serving as a principal, special education director, graduate professor, graduate program director, graduate dean, and longtime superintendent of schools. He was named the Massachusetts Superintendent of the Year; and he completed a distinguished Fulbright program focused on the Japanese educational system through the collegiate level. Dr. Young is the recipient of numerous other honors and recognitions including the General Douglas MacArthur Award for distinguished civilian and military leadership and the Vice Admiral John T. Hayward Award for exemplary scholarship. He holds several graduate degrees including a PhD in educational administration and an EdD in educational psychology.

Dr. Young has served in the U.S. Army and U.S. Army Reserves combined for over 34 years; and he graduated with distinction from the U.S. Air War College, the U.S. Army War College, and the U.S. Navy War College. After completing a series of senior leadership assignments in the U.S. Army Reserves as the commanding officer of the 287th Medical Company (DS), the 405th Area Support Company (DS), the 405th Combat Support Hospital, and the 399th Combat Support Hospital, he transitioned to his current military position as a faculty instructor at the U.S. Army War College in Carlisle, PA. He currently holds the rank of Colonel.

Dr. Young is also a regular presenter at state, national, and international conferences; he has written many books, book chapters, and/or articles on various topics in education, counseling, and psychology. Some of his most recent books include *Potency of the Principalship: Action-Oriented Leadership to Support Student Achievement* (in-press); *The Soul of the Schoolhouse: Cultivating Student Engagement* (in-press); *Captivating Classrooms: Student Engagement at the Heart of School Improvement* (in-press); *Dog Tags to*

Diploma: Understanding and Addressing the Educational Needs of Veterans, Servicemembers, and their Families (in-press); *From Cradle to Classroom: A Guide to Special Education for Young Children* (in-press); *Achieving Results: Maximizing Success in the Schoolhouse* (2018); *From Head to Heart: High Quality Teaching Practices in the Spotlight* (2018); *Stars in the Schoolhouse: Teaching Practices and Approaches that Make a Difference* (2018); *Making the Grade: Promoting Positive Outcomes for Students with Learning Disabilities* (2018); *Paving the Pathway for Educational Success: Effective Classroom Interventions for Students with Learning Disabilities* (2018); *Wrestling with Writing: Effective Strategies for Struggling Students* (2018); *Floundering to Fluent: Reaching and Teaching the Struggling Student* (2018); *Emotions and Education: Promoting Positive Mental Health in Students with Learning* (2018); *From Lecture Hall to Laptop: Opportunities, Challenges, and the Continuing Evolution of Virtual Learning in Higher Education* (2017); *The Power of the Professoriate: Demands, Challenges, and Opportunities in 21st Century Higher Education* (2017); *To Campus with Confidence: Supporting a Successful Transition to College for Students with Learning Disabilities* (2017); *Educational Entrepreneurship: Promoting Public-Private Partnerships for the 21st Century* (2015); *Beyond the Bedtime Story: Promoting Reading Development during the Middle School Years* (2015); *Betwixt and Between: Understanding and Meeting the Social and Emotional Developmental Needs of Students During the Middle School Transition Years* (2014); *Learning Style Perspectives: Impact in the Classroom* (3rd ed., 2014); and *Collapsing Educational Boundaries from Preschool to PhD: Building Bridges Across the Educational Spectrum* (2013); *Transforming Special Education Practices: A Primer for School Administrators and Policy Makers* (2012); and *Powerful Partners in Student Success: Schools, Families and Communities* (2012). He also coauthored several children's books including the popular series I Am Full of Possibilities. Dr. Young may be contacted directly at nyoung1191@aol.com.

Kristen Bonanno-Sotiropoulos, EdD, has worked in education at various levels for more than a dozen years. Her professional career within K–12 public education included roles as a special education teacher and special education administrator at the elementary and middle school levels. After her tenure in K–12, she transitioned to higher education to teach undergraduate and graduate courses as an assistant professor of special education at Springfield College located in Springfield, Massachusetts, and then moved to assistant professor, director of special education programs at Bay Path University. Professor Bonanno-Sotiropoulos received her bachelor of science in liberal studies and elementary education with academic distinction as well as a master of science in moderate disabilities from Bay Path University. She recently completed her EdD in educational leadership and supervision at

American International College, where she focused her research on evidenced-based special education practices. She has coauthored a series of book chapters related to the unique needs of struggling readers as well as how higher education institutions can assist special-needs students with making a successful transition to college. Her current research interests include, among other areas, effective instructional programs and practices to assist learning-disabled students with meeting rigorous academic expectations at all academic levels from preschool to college. Professor Bonanno-Sotiropoulos has become a regular presenter at regional and national conferences and can be reached at kbsotiropoulos@baypath.edu.

Jennifer A. Smolinski has worked in education for more than three years. Her role within higher education includes the creation and directing of the Center for Disability Services and Academic Accommodations at American International College located in Springfield, Massachusetts. She has also taught criminal justice and legal research and writing classes within the field of higher education. Prior to her work at the collegiate level, Attorney Smolinski worked as a solo-practitioner conducting education and disability advocacy as well as representing clients in real estate and business matters.

Attorney Smolinski received a bachelor of arts in anthropology and bachelor of arts in sociology from the University of Connecticut, a master's in psychology and counseling as well as a master's in higher education student affairs from Salem State University and her law degree from Massachusetts School of Law. She is currently an EdD in educational leadership and supervision candidate at American International College, where she is focusing her research on special education and laws to protect students with disabilities in the classroom.

Attorney Smolinski has become a regular presenter educating the faculty, staff, and students at institutes of higher education on disabilities and accommodations at the collegiate level and has presented to local high school special education departments on the transition to college under the Americans with Disabilities Act. She coauthored *Making the Grade: Promoting Positive Outcomes for Students with Learning Disabilities* (2018). She can be reached at Jennifer.Smolinski@aic.edu.

Made in the USA
Columbia, SC
02 December 2018